GET
HEADHUNTED

GET HEADHUNTED

HILTON CATT AND
PATRICIA SCUDAMORE

ORION BUSINESS
BOOKS

This edition published in Great Britain in 2000 by
Orion Business
An imprint of The Orion Publishing Group Ltd
Orion House,
5 Upper St Martin's Lane,
London WC2H 9EA

A CIP catalogue record for this book
is available from the British Library.

ISBN 1 84203 040 X

Typeset by Deltatype Ltd, Birkenhead
Printed and bound in Great Britain
by Clays Ltd, St Ives plc.

CONTENTS

INTRODUCTION

A few words at the beginning 3
Quick quiz 3

**Part one INTRODUCING YOU TO
              HEADHUNTING**

Headhunters: who are they? 14
Why do companies use headhunting? 16
Getting headhunted: what's in it for you? 18
Questions and Answers 19

Part two GETTING ON HEADHUNTERS' NETS

Reasons for not being headhunted 25
Stimulating direct approaches from
  companies 27
Stimulating approach from 'proper' search
  consultants 31
Getting your name onto headhunters'
  files 36
Getting into the files of consultants who carry
  out file search 41
Making file search work for you 51
Marketing yourself effectively by focusing on
  key areas of your skills and experience 58
Availability: making sure that headhunters can
  get hold of you 64
Questions and Answers 70

Part three RECEIVING APPROACHES

Reasons why you are still not being
   headhunted 77
Preparing to take the calls 80
Hearing headhunters out 85
Viewing approach 86
Finding out what the headhunter has to
   offer 87
Finding out where you stand 91
Moving the approach forward 97
After the approach 101
Keeping on good terms with headhunters 106
Questions and Answers 109

Part four NEGOTIATING THE BEST DEAL
FOR YOU

Seeing to it that you don't let the chance go
   by 115
Assessing your bargaining strength 117
Opening the negotiation 121
Controlling the selection process 131
Seeing off competition 137
Moving the negotiation forward 139
Enhancing the package 143
Dealing with enticement 147
Minimising the risks 148
Moving into the future with headhunters 152
Reasons for approaches not turning into
   jobs 154
Questions and Answers 156

Part five GET HEADHUNTED – A MODEL APPROACH

Marketing yourself to headhunters   163
Handling approaches   164
Getting the best deal   164

THE GOLDEN RULES   167

INDEX   179

INTRODUCTION

A FEW WORDS AT THE BEGINNING . . .

Get Headhunted and make doors open for you! This is a tantalising prospect, yet the experience of getting headhunted has different understandings for different people. To some it might mean a contact from someone they know in the trade; to others, the full-blown attentions of a professional executive search consultant.

Get Headhunted explores the different headhunting styles, and the features that go with each. Knowing where you stand when you receive the mysterious telephone call, knowing what to allow for and how to proceed, knowing how to get the best from an approach – these are all subjects we take you through, along with what you can do to enhance your chances of getting headhunted and to enjoy the rich harvest of some of the best opportunities the job market has to offer.

Making approach work for you is an increasingly important part of modern career self-management, hence the inclusion of a book on this subject in the Orion *Career PowerTools* series.

QUICK QUIZ

How do you rate as a headhunting target? Go through these ten questions and tick the answer that most closely approximates your thoughts now. We tell you at the end which ones are the 'best' for an approach situation, but you will have to read the rest of the book to find out why.

Question 1

You receive an approach from your company's biggest competitor. They say they have a job that will interest you and they want to set up a meeting. You know, however, there will be big trouble for you if your company find out you have been talking to the competition. Do you:

A: ☐ Decline?

B: ☐ Tell your company about the approach and that you will be attending the meeting?

C: ☐ Tell your company but agree with them how you should proceed?

D: ☐ Go along to the meeting and keep the approach to yourself?

E: ☐ Tell your company you won't go to the meeting providing they increase your salary?

Question 2

A headhunter refuses to tell you how he got your name. Do you:

A: ☐ View this as a bad sign and have no further dealings with the headhunter?

B: ☐ Make the revelation of his source a condition of any further dealings?

C: ☐ Ask round the office and see if anyone has been talking to the headhunter?

D: ☐ Put some names to the headhunter and ask him to confirm or deny?

E: □ View the source as unimportant and
   proceed to listen to what the
   headhunter has to say?

Question 3

A headhunter asks you if you would be
interested in talking about a position with one
of his clients. You are in a good job with a
good company. Do you:

A: □ Say no?
B: □ Say that you are not interested now but
   that you will go back to the headhunter
   if your circumstances change?
C: □ Go along and listen to what the
   headhunter has to say?
D: □ Tell your company you have received
   an approach and see if it will encourage
   them to give you a rise?
E: □ Suggest the names of colleagues who
   may be more interested?

Question 4

A headhunter approaches you about a position you previously applied for when you saw
it advertised three months ago. On that occasion you didn't get an interview. Do you:

A: □ Keep quiet about your previous
   application?
B: □ Tell the headhunter straight away?
C: □ Wait till you get an interview then tell
   the headhunter?
D: □ Phone the company direct and tell
   them what has happened?
E: □ Say you are not interested in the job?

Question 5

A leading firm of headhunters has put you
through a series of gruelling interviews and

psychological tests but no one has picked up yet that you have recently been disqualified from driving (the question has never been asked). The job is a good job and you don't want to do anything to jeopardise your chances. At this stage you have no idea how the company would view the fact that you have been disqualified. Do you:

A: ☐ Keep it quiet?

B: ☐ Wait till you've been offered the job then mention the disqualification?

C: ☐ Have a quiet word with the company and ask them what they suggest?

D: ☐ Feel you could be getting into a mess and pull out of the approach without giving your reasons?

E: ☐ Draw the headhunters' attention to their omission?

Question 6

Two different headhunters approach you about the same job. Do you?

A: ☐ Go along with both of them on the basis that it doubles your chances?

B: ☐ Tell the second headhunter that you have already received an approach?

C: ☐ Smell a rat and say no to both of them?

D: ☐ Phone up the company and tell them what has happened?

E: ☐ Ask the headhunters to sort it out among themselves?

Question 7

After two previous attempts to headhunt you, a company makes you an offer you find hard to refuse. Unfortunately the company has a

reputation for being a hire and fire organisation and this is why you turned them down
previously. Do you:

A: ☐ Refuse again?

B: ☐ Refuse in the hope they will improve
their offer even further?

C: ☐ Snatch their hand off?

D: ☐ Seek to negotiate a contract
guaranteeing you a fixed minimum
period of employment?

E: ☐ Tell your company about the deal you
have been offered and invite them to
match it?

Question 8

You left a company three years ago after they
repeatedly passed you by for promotion. The
same company is now asking you to go and
see them to talk about an opportunity they
have. Do you:

A: ☐ Tell them to get lost?

B: ☐ Go along and hear what they have to
say?

C: ☐ As B but forewarn them that unless it is
a very good offer you are unlikely to be
interested?

D: ☐ Make it a pre-condition that any re-
engagement would be subject to the
full restoration of your service and
pension rights?

E: ☐ Ask them to set out what they want to
talk to you about in writing so you can
consider it before committing yourself
to a meeting?

Question 9

You have been approached about a very good
job but at this stage the headhunter won't

divulge the identity of his client. The problem
is you know all the companies in the industry
and there are several you would not work for
under any circumstances. The headhunter
now wants you to spend a day at the offices of
his firm undergoing various tests and interviews. Because you don't wish to waste anyone's time, do you:

A: ☐ Tell the headhunter there is no point in
       submitting yourself to tests and
       interviews until you know the identity
       of the client?

B: ☐ See if you can find out who is at the
       back of the approach from your own
       sources?

C: ☐ Pull out?

D: ☐ Give the headhunter a list of the
       companies you would not be prepared
       to work for and ask him to confirm that
       the client is not among them?

E: ☐ Give the headhunter a list as in D
       except leave it to him to decide what
       to do?

Question 10

You find out that a headhunter who has
approached you about a very senior executive
position is associated in some way with an
employment agency dealing with temporary
office staff. Do you:

A: ☐ Smell a rat and pull out?

B: ☐ Demand an explanation?

C: ☐ View the association as irrelevant?

D: ☐ Phone the company to check that the
       headhunter has been given their
       authority to talk to you about the job?

E: ☐ Ask the headhunter to furnish you with
       proof of his or her authority?

How did you get on? The answers we are looking for are:

   1 – C   2 – E   3 – C   4 – B   5 – E

   6 – B   7 – A *(or D if you can afford to take the risk)*

   8 – B   9 – E   10 – C

Why? It's now time to read the book and find out.

INTRODUCING YOU TO HEADHUNTING

Before looking at how to put yourself on the receiving end of headhunters' approaches, it will help you to have an understanding of what headhunting is and how it works. In Part One, we are going to take you on a quick guided tour of the secretive world of executive search and show you a little of what goes on behind the scenes. We will take you through:

- different kinds of headhunting: headhunting done by a consultant and headhunting done by the recruiting company

- different kinds of consultants and what they do; why it's important for you to know the difference

- why companies use professional headhunters; why headhunting has flourished in modern job market conditions

- why so many top jobs are filled by headhunting; what makes headhunting a preferred method of recruitment for companies with senior management positions to fill

- the benefits for you in making yourself a target for headhunters. What you will get from being the one they decide to ring.

....

HEADHUNTERS: WHO ARE THEY?

We can break headhunting down into two main types:

- headhunting done by the employing company
- headhunting done by consultants acting on behalf of the employing company.

Headhunting done by the employing company

This is the familiar poaching that has always gone on, particularly between companies in competing trades. The interest here is usually commercial: Bloggs & Co make a play for Buggins & Co's best sales executive knowing that, if they are successful, not only will they acquire the sales executive's talents, they also stand a good chance of nobbling some of Buggins & Co's top accounts.

Though, by its very nature, headhunting done by companies is hard to quantify, it is certainly true to say that most headhunting falls into this category. The headhunter will be an executive of the company or someone close to them. The target of the approach will almost always be someone they know.

Headhunting done by consultants

Here, there is a distinction between:

- headhunting done by consultants who locate candidates to match their clients' specifications by using their knowledge and contacts (this is most people's understanding of headhunting, and so from here on we will refer to it as **proper search**).

- headhunting done from a database where consultants are matching their clients' specifications with candidates they have on file (hence the term **file search**).

There are three important differences between proper search and file search:

- **The competencies required to carry out the search.** Proper search calls for a high degree of business understanding and lateral thinking ability as well as good connections (networks). These competencies may or may not be present in a consultancy that deals largely in file search.

- **The time scales involved.** A client company would normally expect a file search to be completed within 24–48 hours (the time it takes to do the search and check with matched candidates to see if they are still 'available'). Proper search, in contrast, is a very time-consuming business. Putting out feelers and waiting for feedback, then vetting the feedback can take weeks and even months to finalise.

- **The price.** Typically file search costs around 15–20% of the annual salary for the job but, more important for you to know, the normal arrangement is for the consultant's fee only to become payable when someone starts. Proper search, on the other hand, commands a much higher fee structure (around a third of the annual starting salary plus the consultant's expenses). A common arrangement here is for the fee to be payable in instalments, e.g. a third at the beginning of the assignment, a third on submission of a shortlist and the final third when a candidate starts.

....

WHY DO COMPANIES USE HEADHUNTING?

Headhunting is just one of the recruitment options open to companies when they have vacancies to fill. There are others of course – notably advertising. So why is it they choose headhunting? Why, in particular do they go for headhunting as the preferred way of filling top management jobs. The following chief executives explain their reasons:

> 'When we have a vacancy the kind of person we hope to fill it won't necessarily be looking for another job – hence we can't bank on an ad in a newspaper doing the trick for us, so we go to a headhunter.'

> 'We find we don't have the time to deal with sifting through hundreds of replies to advertisements. It's far easier for us to pick up the phone and ask a headhunter to come up with a shortlist of people for us.'

> 'Taking on square pegs, particularly into senior management positions, is a constant source of worry to us. We feel far more comfortable with people we know or people who are recommended to us by consultants. Any Tom, Dick or Harriet can reply to an advertisement.'

*'We are in the business of sourcing people
with scarce and very sought-after skills.
Advertising doesn't work for us. As far as we
are concerned, the only answer is search.'*

*'We have very firm ideas on the kind of
people we want to bring into top
management positions. We find the best way
of finding these people is to headhunt them.'*

What's interesting about these responses is
how they illustrate the extent to which modern job market conditions have contributed to
the growth of headhunting as a method of
recruiting, notably:

- the downsizing and the delayering that
  has gone on in many companies and that
  has led to fewer people at management
  level. This means fewer managers to deal
  with the time-consuming, hands-on
  aspects of recruitment such as sifting
  through applications, carrying out
  interviews, checking references, etc.

- coupled with this, the demise of the
  human resources (personnel) functions in
  many companies – meaning responsibility
  for organising recruitment has been
  turned over to people who have neither
  the time nor the experience and training
  to do it properly. In these situations
  headhunting provides a short-cut

- increased awareness of the consequences
  of making bad selection decisions: the
  damage this can do to the business
  particularly if the bad choice is a senior
  job holder; the difficulty of removing bad
  choices; the increased likelihood these
  days of litigation ensuing from dismissals

- the scarcity of people with key skills (a
  reflection of under-investment in training

in our recent recession-plagued past); the commonly held view that acquiring such people calls for 'something special'.

....

GETTING HEADHUNTED: WHAT'S IN IT FOR YOU?

To sum up so far:

- headhunting is big
- it's getting bigger
- a lot of good jobs are filled by headhunting
- you can't afford to miss out on it.

But there's another benefit to being head-hunted, and it is this: every good job that is advertised these days attracts large numbers of applicants and this reflects two further aspects of the slim-line flattened down corporate world we live in:

- good job opportunities are not that easy to come by

- there are a large number of people who see their career paths as being blocked off or not progressing in the way they would like them to progress.

Given this imbalance in supply and demand, competition is always going to be a major factor with good jobs that are advertised – and how much competition will depend largely on:

- how good is good
- how much advertising exposure the job is given.

With the latter, whether the job has been

advertised in local or national newspapers, or in professional or trade journals, or in all or most of these will determine whether the response is measurable in dozens, hundreds or thousands. Whatever the count, it goes without saying that with advertised (visible market) jobs you will face an uphill challenge even to get on the interview list.

Contrast this with positions filled by headhunting where consultants are often putting up only a handful of candidates for their clients to consider. Indeed, it is not unusual in these situations to find yourself the only runner in a one-horse race; this is commoner than you think, especially where companies are doing their own headhunting (where just one individual known to the company has been targeted and approached).

GOLDEN RULE 1

See what's in it for you.

Questions and answers

Is headhunting confined to top jobs?

Q I've always associated headhunting with top jobs (chief executives, directors, etc.) but am I right in thinking this? How far down the ladder do headhunters go?

A Broadly speaking anyone with sought-after skills is a potential target for headhunting and this includes people with manual (craft) skills as well as various types of technicians. You would be right, however, in assuming that most proper search goes on in the upper salary echelons. Because of its cost and time consumption, proper search is usually confined to very senior management or board-level appointments.

Executive search and selection consultants

Q What do I gather about a business that styles itself 'executive search and selection consultants'?

A Because of the looseness with which terminology is used in this field, almost anything. In the strict sense, it describes a consultancy where search of one sort of another is combined with doing selection assignments for companies, e.g. advertising positions, carrying out preliminary interviews and submitting shortlists of candidates.

In the next chapter we will see how candidates seeking to be headhunted can turn these multi-faceted consultancies to their advantage.

TICK YOUR PROGRESS
....

- ✓ Most headhunting is done by companies and most approaches are from people who work for companies (not consultants). Often these people will be people known to you.

- ✓ Consultants divide into consultants who do proper search and consultants who put forward lists of candidates from their files. Some consultants do both.

- ✓ Some companies use headhunters because they don't have the resources or expertise to deal with recruitment themselves.

- ✓ Some of the best jobs are filled by headhunting.

✓ Approach is where you face least competition.

✓ Getting headhunted is something you should be seeking to encourage.

GETTING ON HEADHUNTERS' NETS

On the face of it, getting headhunted is an event over which you have no control. The mystery telephone call comes straight out of the blue and has no apparent connection with anything you have instigated. Yet there are steps you can take to boost your chances of getting headhunted. In Part Two we will look at:

- why people don't get headhunted – a checklist of the common reasons

- stimulating approaches from companies – how to develop your professional networks

- how to get your name on headhunters' files

- adding to your skills and experience and making yourself a more attractive target for headhunters; marketing what you've got

- making it easy for headhunters to contact you; paying attention to your availability.

....

REASONS FOR NOT BEING HEADHUNTED

'I have never been headhunted and I have a feeling that this is because I don't mix in the right circles. Apart from changing my entire life-style, I don't see there is a fat lot I can do about it.'

The reasons why people don't get headhunted

usually have nothing to do with their social habits. If you fall into the category of 'never been headhunted' run through this checklist of possible explanations. Do this before you start jumping to too many conclusions about your failings:

- Are you young, newly qualified or relatively inexperienced? Companies use headhunting to source people with skills and experience they can't acquire by other means. Hence, if you are in the 'still learning' bracket don't expect to be the subject of too many, or any, approaches. Your turn will come later.

- What's the economy performing like at the moment? The amount of headhunting that goes on traditionally takes a nose-dive during recessionary periods. Not only will companies have fewer vacancies, they will tend to fill them by other means. For example, redundant executives will be using their networking skills to find jobs for themselves, so companies will be receiving approaches (rather than having to make them). The message here is: don't expect to be headhunted during a slump.

- Have you been on the job market recently? If not, then the chances are your details won't be on any consultants' files. For corrective action you can take, see pages 41 to 51.

- What's your employment history like? Have you left previous jobs on good terms or has there been a cloud hanging over your head? What would colleagues and former colleagues think of you? A lot of headhunting stems from your name being put in the hat by someone who knows you or someone who has known you in the past. Clearly, they won't be inclined to do this if they have got misgivings about you. The moral here is that being headhunted is a less likely outcome if, for any reason, you don't pass the person perfect and work perfect test. Read what we've got to say about the *lifelong interview* on page 31.

- Are you easy to contact or are you one of those people headhunters find impossible to catch up with? If you fall into the latter category you are probably not aware of it. Carry out an availability audit along the lines we suggest on pages 68 to 70. Don't fall into the trap of never being there when headhunters want to speak to you.

....

STIMULATING DIRECT APPROACHES FROM COMPANIES

There are six key features of companies doing their own headhunting:

- It is more common than headhunting by consultants.

- The target is almost always someone who is known to the company – either directly or through a close associate (e.g. a professional adviser).

- The approach is usually made by an executive of the company – often the person who knows the targeted individual.

- The 'comfort' factor weighs heavily with companies who choose this method of recruitment. The fact that they have knowledge of the individual and the individual's work is a point strongly in his or her favour.

- In these situations, it's not uncommon to find that only one individual is being approached.

- Apart from the time spent, there is no cost to the company (i.e. no consultants' fees).

Now we'll take a look at a case study and see how two real people fared when it came to being headhunted by a company. Think about what lessons you can draw from their experiences.

CASE STUDY: RYAN AND SIMON

Paul is the director in charge of the fasteners division of a large engineering company. The division is bringing a new factory on stream in six months' time and Paul is looking for a factory manager to run the fledgling operation. With no suitable internal candidates, Paul has turned his thoughts to people he knows.

The first of these is Ryan. Ryan works for Paul's old company so Paul knows him well (at one point, Ryan was Paul's assistant). Paul has heard via the grapevine that Ryan is not very happy with his current situation and feels certain he will jump at the chance of running the new factory. The problem for Paul is that at the time they worked together Ryan had a tendency to go to pieces under pressure. If Ryan is still inclined the same way, Paul realises the situation may become difficult when teething troubles with new machines start to rear their ugly heads – as sooner or later they will.

The other possible is Simon. Simon is a young production engineer who works for a competitor and who is known to Paul only through membership of a fasteners industry technical working party. Despite their slight acquaintance, Paul is very taken with Simon: he is relatively young for the position, but he handles himself well and his technical knowledge is good.

After careful consideration, and with some genuine regret, Paul decides to give Ryan a miss. Too much is at stake with the new factory and Paul feels he needs someone in charge whom he can rely on not to flap when things start going wrong. In this respect, Ryan's track record is worrying. Simon, on the other hand, has no such history as far as Paul is aware.

Paul reflects briefly on whether he should advertise the factory manager's job. The rigmarole of sifting through hundreds of applications does not appeal so, on that basis, he decides to sound out Simon first. He picks up the phone and, without disclosing what he wants to talk to him about, he invites Simon to join him for a beer and a sandwich.

Negotiations with Simon may yet founder, but the important points to reflect on here are:

- how being well known to Paul worked to Ryan's disadvantage
- how a negative aspect of Ryan's character and job performance was held against him, even though the experience dated from a long way back
- how people like Paul play it safe – especially when there is a lot at stake
- how by controlling the impressions he fed out to Paul (intentionally or not), Simon found himself on the receiving end of an interesting approach.

Professional networking

The case study illustrates:

- how professional networks access you to direct approaches from companies
- how it only works where you have made the right impressions.

Professional networking is a subject all on its own, and one explored in another book in the Orion *PowerTools* series called *Powerful Networking*, by John Lockett. One common flaw in the way a lot of people approach networking is they put all their effort into extending networks (getting onto networking terms with more and more people), while paying scant attention to making their networks work for them. There are a couple of things worth bearing in mind while reading this book:

- Professional networks are a natural consequence of being in a career: they consist of people you work with, people you have worked with in the past and a mix of trade/professional contacts. Networks don't need artificial growth stimulants. Size wise, they take care of themselves.

- How your professional networks perform for you – in this instance, whether or not they enhance your chances of being headhunted – depends entirely on the impressions you create among the people you have dealings with in the day-to-day course of your work.

GOLDEN RULE 2

Cultivate your networks.

The lifelong interview

A particularly important aspect of good professional networking is controlling the messages
that you feed out about yourself and – as we
saw in the case of Ryan and Paul – this is
hardest with people you work with closely.
Yes, familiarity also has the habit of breeding
contempt, but think of it this way: every day
you go to work, view it in the same way that
you would view going for an important interview. Put on the gloss and don't broadcast
your flaws (we've all got flaws) but, most of all,
remember you're not doing this for just 45–60
minutes in front of someone you've never met
before. Hopefully you now understand why
we describe this integral part of professional
networking as your *lifelong interview*. Remember this term because you will hear it again.

....

STIMULATING APPROACH
FROM 'PROPER' SEARCH
CONSULTANTS

You will recall from what we said in Part One
that professional headhunters (consultants)
fall into these two main types:

- *proper searchers* – those who use their
  contacts, knowledge and lateral thinking
  ability to target suitable candidates
- *file searchers* – those who make matches
  with their clients' specifications from
  details of candidates they hold on a
  database.

In this section we are going to consider proper
searchers (some would call them the true
headhunters) and look at:

- how they go about their business.
- what you can do to enhance your chances of being on the receiving end of an approach from one.

First, we'll list some key features of proper search:

- Because of the time and cost involved, the use of proper search is largely confined to the top end of the job market, typically to board level appointments. This means from your point of view that approaches from proper search consultants are particularly worth encouraging.

- Companies commissioning proper search do so because they believe it gives them access to people they wouldn't have knowledge of otherwise (the famous mystique of search consultants). Comfort will also be drawn from the fact that consultants' reputations are on the line with any candidates that they put forward.

- Only in a small number of cases will the target be known to the searcher at the outset. The same applies vice versa.

- Though a number of people may be approached, only a few will be submitted to the client in the form of a shortlist.

How proper search consultants work

How do proper search consultants draw up their lists of people to make contact with and, the hundred thousand dollar question, what can you do to increase the chances of your name appearing on one of these lists?

Every search assignment is different and no two searchers operate in exactly the same way. Below, some searchers describe their methods.

'Over the years I've developed a network of contacts: people in all walks of life whose opinions I respect and who I regularly pump for names.'

'Providing they work in the right sector, a valuable source of names is candidates we have had dealings with in the past. Often they can put us onto someone they know or someone who knows someone else. This is a good way of getting the ball rolling.'

'Our client list can be very useful to us. We land a search assignment from firm X then use our contacts in firms Y and Z to give us names. Frequently these will be the names of former employees or trade contacts so no conflict of interest is involved.'

'Bodies like professional institutions or trade associations can be very helpful. At the local level, they form little networks of people who are known to one another – networks that we can tap into.'

'If we are struggling with an assignment because the job is in a sector where we don't have too many contacts, we might resort to cold calling a few people. The people we go for will be people whose job functions indicate that they are likely to have the kind of skills and experience we are seeking. Even if they are not interested in a move themselves, they may be able to put us onto someone they know, e.g. present and past colleagues, people with similar skills and experience.'

We could go on with these little snippets of information from behind the scenes, but a picture is already starting to emerge: that these true headhunters mostly get their leads from tapping into other people's networks. They pinpoint people who are likely to have the right contacts and take it from there.

Why should anyone want to help a head-hunter in this way? For the same reason that you will be following suit: because you want to keep on the right side of the headhunters; because some day one of them may have a job that's right up your street and the last thing you will want is to miss out because you've been crossed off the call list. We have much more to say on the subject of cultivating headhunters later in the book.

But the point for you to focus on here is not the headhunter's astute way of making money but how your involvement in the chain of contacts is dictated by your lifelong interview skills. To get yourself onto the headhunter's list of people to approach, someone has to know you and, more importantly, the same someone has to have sufficient confidence in you to feel moved to put your name forward. Clearly, they are not going to do this if they know of blemishes on your character or if they associate you with someone whose perform-ance is substandard. Their reputation with the headhunter is just as much on the line as the headhunter's reputation is with his or her client. You must therefore be seen as *person perfect* and *work perfect* and this is especially the case with top-drawer jobs.

Visibility

Another source of targets for headhunters is from information that is held in the public domain. For example, if you are a director of a company, your name will appear in its published report and accounts. If a company's performance has been good, a headhunter will be able to see at a glance the names of those who have been responsible for the success.

Bringing yourself to the attention of headhunters by heightening your public profile sometimes happens unintentionally. In the following two case studies, senior managers relate their experiences.

CASE STUDY: MILES

'My company recently received an award for quality of service to customers and it fell on me to attend the presentation. The press were present at this gathering and, as a result, my picture appeared in the business news section of the local paper. Lo and behold, over the next fortnight, I received no less than four calls from headhunters.'

CASE STUDY: LISA

'Because of an upsurge in staff turnover my company recently embarked on a very upbeat recruitment advertising campaign and, as human resources manager, it was my name that appeared in the advertisements as the person to whom CVs should be addressed. I was inundated with telephone calls including two from headhunters asking me if I would be interested in positions they had with clients in the recruitment industry.'

What these experiences illustrate is the importance of visibility as a vehicle for getting onto headhunters' nets, and more important still, if the visibility is going to work for you, it has to associate you with the right kind of things. In Miles's case the right kind of thing was the excellence of his company's service to customers; in Lisa's, a series of upbeat recruitment advertisements. Conversely, visibility associated with the wrong kind of things won't get you anywhere. For instance, if the report in the press was to say the company had chalked up record losses since you took over as managing director, don't expect too many headhunters to be ringing you up!

| GOLDEN RULE 3 |

Be visible.

....

GETTING YOUR NAME ONTO HEADHUNTERS' FILES

There are two quite separate challenges here:

- getting your name onto the files of proper search consultants
- getting your name onto the files of consultants who carry out file search.

Getting onto the files of proper search consultants

The files of proper search consultants tend to consist of:

- people who have been trawled on previous search assignments (i.e. people who were not placed)
- people who have been recommended (people kept on file because they may have potential for placement in the future).

Proper search consultants will delve into their files at the same time as sourcing candidates by their more normal route of using their contacts and know-how. The key differences between proper search consultants' files and the files of consultants who do standard file searches are:

- **size** – proper search consultants' files will be small by comparison – the problem of making your file stand out from the rest is not therefore one that should arise

- **selectivity** – proper search consultants are notoriously choosy about who they keep on file – you can't register with a proper search consultancy in the same way that you can register with an agency-type firm of recruitment consultants.

This choosiness has given rise to the legend that the only way of getting onto proper search consultants' files is by having the right connections or mixing in certain social circles. In other words the Joe and Jane Ordinaries of this world needn't bother, because they will find the doors slammed shut.

There is a question at the end of this chapter that deals with the alleged impenetrability of proper search consultants' exclusive worlds, but the message at this stage is don't be put off by the popular image. The reality is often far more mundane and the dos and don'ts of getting your foot round proper search consultants' doors boil down to quite basic considerations of who they are and what they do.

Don't, therefore, pepper proper search consultants with unsolicited cvs: the chances are they will end up in the bin, unread along with all the other cvs they receive. Proper search consultants are not agencies and trying to treat them as such is not a winning strategy.

Do, on the other hand, play proper search consultants at their own game, by which we mean use your connections to open the doors for you.

Plan of action

- Have you ever received an approach from a proper search consultant? If so, can you recall his or her name and the consultancy with which he or she was connected?

- Do you know anyone who has been approached by a proper search consultant? There is an increasing likelihood these days that someone from among your circle of friends and professional contacts has had this privilege. If so, find out the name of the consultant involved.

- If you get the name of a headhunter from someone else, check before you go any further that the headhunter deals with people at your level or with your range of skills. It is common to find that headhunters deal in certain professions or types of jobs and it is important to know that you are going to be talking to the right person.

- use the telephone to make contact with proper search consultants.

- Be quick to grab their attention by identifying your connection ('I got your name from Charles Mattox; you placed him in a job with Bloggs & Associates at the end of last year ...').

- State quickly who you are, where you are coming from and what, in career terms, you are trying to achieve. Don't try to embellish what you are saying with long lists of your achievements or self-praise. Professional headhunters have heard it all before and won't be impressed.

- There are a few possible outcomes here: the headhunter will suggest setting up a meeting (a very good sign that there is something on the anvil or that you have stirred up interest), *or* he/she will ask you to send in a cv, *or* the headhunter will tell you that he/she has nothing to interest you at the moment.

- If you are requested to send in a cv, ask the headhunter if he or she would like it faxed. If the answer is yes, take this as another good sign. (If you fax in a cv make sure to follow up with a hard copy in first-class post the same day – faxes crinkle and fade with age so they won't look good when they have been picked up and put down a few times. Remember, in dealing with proper search consultants you are tendering to an industry that is based on impressions and a dog-eared cv clearly won't do much for you on the impressions front.)

- If you are told there is nothing doing then leave the door open for future contact ('Is it OK if I ring you again in three months' time to see if things have changed?'). Don't necessarily read a 'nothing doing' response as meaning the headhunter isn't interested in you.

- Prick up your ears if the headhunter tells you he or she can't help (period). Disengage because you are probably talking to the wrong headhunter.

The underlying features to this phone call are as follows:

- The association with Charles Mattox should strike up an immediate and good rapport. By the nature of the work (and in contrast with people who operate in the volume-driven file search business) proper search consultants don't get involved in that many assignments over the course of a year, hence the name Charles Mattox will (a) be remembered, and (b) be associated with something pleasant (the big fat commission the consultant earned from Bloggs & Associates for Charles's placement).

- Like everyone else, proper search consultants are in business to make money. In their case, they only make money out of people they can place with their clients and, nothing to do with snobbery or the old boy or girl net, their interest in you will be dictated entirely by this criterion. If, for example, you are an expert in plastics and if the consultancy specialises in finding people with IT skills, their interest in you is going to be nil.

- The telephone is the proper search consultants' natural medium and so you will establish a far better rapport by ringing them (better than writing or sending e-mails etc.).

....

GETTING ONTO THE FILES OF CONSULTANTS WHO CARRY OUT FILE SEARCH

The key features to headhunting from file search are:

- The competencies required to do file search are much lower than the competencies required to do proper search. Preliminary file search is often done by computer.

- Companies commission file search because it offers them speedy results. Shortlists of candidates can normally be put together in 24–48 hours.

- Fees for file search are lower than fees for proper search. More importantly, the common arrangement is for the fee not to become payable until someone starts. This means the company commissioning a file search has the opportunity to view candidates on offer before they part with any money (a good selling point).

- File search is used across the board – from unskilled jobs up to senior management posts. Its usage tends to tail off the further up the ladder you go. Proper search and advertising are the more preferred methods of recruitment for jobs in the over £50k per annum bracket.

Can you afford to ignore file search as a source of approach? Unless you happen to be in the very narrow band of top jobs the answer is emphatically 'no'. Why? Listen to what a leading business figure has to say about file search:

*'As a first shot we spin all our vacancies
through the handful of recruitment
consultants we regularly use and get them to
do a file search. If we can pick up someone
suitable from an exercise such as this then
it's good news because it saves us the bother
of advertising or waiting for [proper] search
consultants to get their acts together. If not,
all we've lost is a couple of days and, best of
all, it's cost us nothing.'*

The key points to pick out are:

- the quickness and no placement/no fee
  aspects of file search impress a lot of
  companies – particularly companies in
  a hurry

- these days there are more and more
  companies in a hurry and the slow pace
  at which recruitment by advertising or
  proper search moves doesn't appeal to
  them one bit

- being trawled out of a recruitment
  consultant's files in a file search often
  accesses jobs *before* they are advertised
  or put out to proper search consultants.
  It means in effect that you can get
  a preview of what's on the market.

Different types of consultants who do file search

*'Search consultants, selection consultants,
recruitment consultants, employment
agencies: is there any difference between
them? If I want to be headhunted whose files
do I need to be on?'*

The difficulty in penetrating the terminology
is entirely understandable, not least because

consultants operating in the employment field apply these labels to themselves fairly indiscriminately.

We'll start, therefore, with a few definitions:

Selection consultant This is someone who carries out a selection assignment for a company, normally by advertising a position under the consultancy's name and carrying out some of the initial selection procedures (e.g. preliminary interviews, psychometric testing of shortlist candidates etc.). Selection consultants offer cover to client companies who wish their identities to remain confidential. They also offer expertise (which these companies may not have).

Search consultant This is someone who locates suitable candidates by using his or her knowledge, contacts and lateral thinking ability (proper search). Search consultants offer confidentiality, expertise and access to candidates who would not otherwise apply for positions.

Recruitment consultant This is a term properly applied to someone who works for an employment agency (see below) where candidates are sourced largely from file search (candidates who are registered with them) or by limited advertising (e.g. small ads in newspapers).

Employment agency This is a generic term to describe any kind of business offering to supply staff on a permanent or temporary basis. For image reasons (and to distance themselves from the familiar temp-oriented high street pop in shop type operation) employment agencies specialising in professional and/or executive staff frequently choose not to describe themselves as such. Here is where you might find potentially misleading terminology used (e.g. 'management search and selection consultants' where the business does neither).

So to sum up, what we are looking at here is how to get your names on the files of recruitment consultants who:

- may not call themselves recruitment consultants
- work for employment agencies who may not call themselves employment agencies.

Confused? Wait till you've gone through *Yellow Pages* and seen how many employment agencies are listed. In many large towns and cities the numbers can run into hundreds, so the first task you've got is to find a way of picking out the right ones.

Choosing firms of recruitment consultants with which to register

'I've had my name on the files of umpteen recruitment consultants for nearly two years. All I have had so far is one telephone call about a job that turned out to be completely unsuitable for me.'

To be any use to you in terms of enhancing your chances of being headhunted, firms of recruitment consultants have to meet three criteria:

- first and foremost, they must deal with the category of people you fit into. For instance, consultants who specialise in people with accountancy qualifications won't be any good to you if you are a solicitor or a software designer
- they must have a good client base

- they must be proficient – meaning they
  must be capable of matching you with
  the right kind of opportunities (with
  recruitment consultants proficiency is
  never a foregone conclusion!).

Knowing whether a firm of recruitment consultants handles the kind of appointments
that would interest you isn't always easy.
Occasionally the names are a give away
(names like 'Engineering Design Personnel' for
example), or they will have block advertisements in business directories that list out what
they do. More often than not, however, you
will encounter names like Jones, Smith &
Associates that will leave you guessing. As to
client base, you will have no idea, of course
(recruitment consultants understandably play
their client lists very close to their chests).
Similarly with proficiency: you will have no
clue as to whether they are any good or not
until you have had some experience of how
they perform.

Choosing the right firms of recruitment consultants

- Are there any obvious 'big names', i.e.
  major players, in recruitment in whatever
  occupational group you belong to? The
  point to 'big names' is that, irrespective of
  how good they are, they tend to
  command large chunks of the market –
  meaning, from your point of view, that
  companies will tend to go to them simply
  because of their size and prominence.
  Incidentally, big isn't necessarily beautiful
  in the world of recruitment consultants.
  'Big names' figure in some of the worst
  disaster stories we have heard, so stand by
  to have to grin and bear it. Their share of
  the market and how you could profit by

it is the reason why you will be putting up with them.

- Do you have any friends or colleagues in the same profession who have had recent experience of dealing with firms of recruitment consultants? If so, see if you can pick their brains for leads.

- Scan the job ads in the newspapers and see which firms of consultants seem to be advertising for people like you.

- Do you know any human resources (personnel) managers or anyone else who has worked in the employment field? Such people are often mines of information on recruitment consultants operating in the local area.

- Don't register with too many recruitment consultants at the same time (six is a sensible maximum) – otherwise you may find their attentions hard to handle.

- Judge recruitment consultants by their performance over a six-month period. If you have received no approaches from them in that time – and providing the economy is not in recession – take it to indicate that their client base is weak. If the approaches you have received are for the wrong kinds of jobs then take it as a reflection of their proficiency. In either case disengage from the consultants by simply asking for your name to be taken off their files. Find another firm of consultants to register with – this is one of the advantages of having so much choice.

How do you go about registering with a firm of recruitment consultants? This is the easy part. Often it only takes a phone call. There will probably be a registration form to fill in and, depending on the consultancy, you may have to attend an interview or undergo a psychometric test. Later on in this chapter (pages 51 to 63) we will be looking at self-marketing and how to project your skills and experience to people like recruitment consultants – including how to fill in registration forms to enhance your chances of being the one whose name pops out of the files at the right time.

Getting onto the files of consultants who carry out both proper search and file search

At this juncture we'll introduce one of the common creatures that swim in the seas of employment consultancy: the hybrid – the consultancy that deals in a mix of activities: proper search, file search, and carrying out selection assignments. The consultant in these cases will be someone who swaps hats as and when business dictates.

To illustrate what these businesses have to offer people like you who are seeking to enhance their chances of being headhunted we'll look at an example of the typical kind of advertisement placed by a firm of consultants engaged on a selection assignment (over the page).

The little tag 'search and selection' alongside FFF's logo could mean anything. It could mean, for example, they do search (proper search) and selection, or file search and selection, or all three – or it could be just a fancy title for a business that deals in selection only, or it may be little more than a glorified advertising agency posing as a front for one of its clients. But the point to drawing your attention to consultants who do a little of

SALES HIGH FLIERS

£40k OTE + prestige car and benefits
Home Counties

Our client, a global market leader in the field of telecommunications systems, is looking to expand its team of sales professionals with the appointment of three key account executives based in the London area. The company's ambitious growth plans are backed by a commitment to being at the leading edge of technology and developing bespoke solutions to customers' needs.

To qualify for one of these positions you will need to have:

> at least two years' experience of selling within telecommunications or a related field

> a hands-on approach with the ability to focus on customers' problems

> the ability to work in highly integrated teams alongside technical and design personnel

> flair and energy to push through schemes and develop sales to your territory.

The company offers a substantial package with a high basic salary and many attractive fringe benefits (commensurate with a major player in the industry).

If the challenge of moving into the big league appeals to you send a copy of your cv quoting reference no FFF/OIN99 to:
Jane Frobisher, Frobisher Fish Fiddler & Associates, FFF House, High Street, Anytown on Thames, Bucks AT99 9XX

(FFF)⌐ search and selection

everything (of which Frobisher Fish Fiddler & Associates may be one) is to highlight the potential spin-offs from having your name on their files.

Jane Frobisher, the consultant whose name appears in the advertisement is, on this occasion, carrying out a selection exercise for a specific client. At some point in the future, however, she may be asked to do a headhunting (proper search) assignment for an entirely different client. In her search for suitable candidates, Jane is in the first instance going to look in FFF's own database, which by now will include the sales high fliers who applied to be key account executives but who, for one reason or another, were not successful. To emphasise the point a little further, let's hear what one of these consultants who wears a number of hats has to say on the subject of his firm's database:

> 'Doing selection assignments for clients provides us with great free advertising. Not only does it get our name into prominence in newspapers, but it also brings in large numbers of candidates. Seeing that in most cases our clients are only interested in taking on one person, the bulk of these candidates find their way onto our files and, in the fullness of time, we are able to place many of them elsewhere. This is good business for us because sourcing candidates in this way has no cost for us.'

Dealing with search and selection consultants

- Keep your eyes open for these umbrella organisations.

- Pick them out of the business directories or spot their ads in the papers.

- Apply the usual test of making sure the consultancy deals with people in your category. See what the entry in the business directory tells you or see whether their ads in the paper match your skills.

- Be aware that some businesses that style themselves 'search and selection' are little more than advertising agencies offering a front to their clients via a confidential reply service. The important point for you is that such businesses are unlikely to maintain databases of candidates.

- Applying for jobs advertised by search and selection consultants is a clear path onto their books. Alternatively, if the job being advertised doesn't appeal to you, ring them up and ask what you have to do to get on their files. (Incidentally you should be able to pick up from this conversation if the business is just an advertising agency – they won't have the facilities to register you and, if this is the answer you get, disengage.)

- If the business is a genuine search and selection consultancy, and the prospect is there for them to make money out of you, you will find them more than eager to get you on their files. If there is resistance, then it is likely to be because they genuinely feel they are not going to be able to help you (e.g. because they do not deal with people with your skills). Listen to what they are saying: don't push yourself onto consultancies who resist you, because there is no point.

- Don't get bogged down with splitting hairs with consultants over what kind of search activities they are involved in. Over the phone they may be cagey with you anyway and, as we have seen, the definitions of what does or does not constitute 'search' and 'headhunting' are so blurred you may not learn a lot from their answers.

- Proceed as you would with a firm of standard recruitment consultants (pages 51 to 58). Review their performance in exactly the same way.

....

MAKING FILE SEARCH WORK FOR YOU

There are two main areas of difficulty to focus on when considering how to make yourself a target for headhunting from file search. The first is the one we have dealt with in the preceding section: how to identify file searchers and distinguish between those who are going to be useful to you and those who are not. The second and more crucial area of difficulty is how to make file search work for you – how to ensure your name pops out of the file at the right time.

Recruitment consultants' files are typified by their size. The more candidates they have on file, the more chances they have of finding suitable people to match their clients' needs, and so the more chances they have of making some money for themselves.

The sheer volume of people on file, particularly with the larger consultancies, is what presents you with the biggest single challenge in making file search work for you: to put it bluntly, how do you make your name stand out from the crowd?

Filling in registration forms

When you register with a firm of recruitment consultants you may have to attend an interview, you may even have to sit a psychometric test, but what you will certainly have to do is fill in one of their forms.

Too little attention is paid to the forms people are asked to fill in when they register with firms of recruitment consultants. This is a pity for two reasons:

- the form is the basis of the permanent information that is kept on file. What is said during the course of an interview may be forgotten unless it is written down, but what appears on the form is there for as long as you remain on the consultancy's files

- a photocopy of the form is frequently what goes forward to interested employers, i.e. the person viewing what you have put on the form may be your next boss.

How *not to* complete your form

- Don't just refer to your cv. People filling in registration forms for firms of recruitment consultants quickly spot that many of the questions tally with information that is given in their carefully prepared cvs. Feeling either too lazy to list out the information again or that the consultant's form affords insufficient space they simply write 'see cv' alongside the questions. Don't do this. Some consultancies may have the patience to ask you to fill the form in again but, in dealing with businesses that are results-oriented and volume driven (more on this in a moment) you will be running the risk of having your form filed through the shredding machine. There is the celebrated case of the bright spark who completed a registration form by writing 'see cv' in every blank space then forgot to include it. By definition, he or she remains anonymous!

- Don't write in coloured inks (or, worse still, use a pencil). Colours don't photo-copy well or, if your details have to be faxed to a prospective employer, your form could end up illegible (again people in a hurry and with lots of other forms to look at will be tempted to put it in the bin).

- Don't scribble. Either because you have a dislike for filling in forms or because you think the form is for internal use only or because you are too busy, you may be tempted to dash the form off in a couple of minutes – don't! Really untidy forms or forms with crossings out or studded with big blobs of correcting fluid run the risk of finding their way into the shredding machine.

- Don't use the form to exercise your wit or express your opinions. An example of the latter is the candidate who, on finding that a registration form only allowed him two lines to list out his impressive array of qualifications, wrote in the space: 'How can I get details of the exams I have passed in here? This form has obviously been designed for morons.' Again the risk is that the form will end up in the shredding pile or, if it does get passed through to a prospective employer, the impression is of someone who is potentially difficult to deal with. Either outcome won't do you a lot of good on the getting headhunted front.

- Don't answer questions vaguely or imprecisely. An example is the question that asks you to describe what kinds of jobs you are looking for. Questions like these are put there to ensure your form is processed correctly (that it will be slotted into the right section of the files and that the retrieval systems will work). Answers such as 'anything' or 'open to discussion' therefore invite problems. People who complain that recruitment consultants approach them with unsuitable opportunities often have to look no further than their own lack of specification for an explanation.

How *to* complete your form

Now we'll turn the accent from the negative to the positive and look at what you should be doing when you are confronted with one of these forms and in particular what will help bring you to the fore in a file search; what, in turn, will enhance your chances of being headhunted. For the purpose of this exercise it will help you to make the following assumptions:

- any recruitment consultants you deal with will be heavily results-oriented. They will be driven not just by the wish to keep their customers happy but also by the need to earn decent commissions for themselves. Their minds will be sharply focused on the fact that the sales value of their efforts is zero until they place someone in a job. As a consequence they will have little time for people who they see as hard to please or difficult to deal with. Smart Alecs or anyone else with the propensity for rubbing their clients up the wrong way certainly won't appeal.

- A recruitment consultancy is a busy place where new registrations will be subject to bulk processing. Whether these registrations will be processed correctly or not will depend entirely on the extent to which candidates can convey where they are coming from and what they are seeking to achieve in one quick read of their paperwork (this is known as their *accessibility*). Candidates who fail the 'one quick read' test will find themselves cast into outer darkness (the wrong file or the shredding machine or onto the 'don't know' pile, i.e. places from which they are unlikely ever to be retrieved).

- File search will be conducted by computer or manually by someone who may not have a complete understanding of what it is that you do or the terminology you use.

Admittedly, this paints a stark picture of what life is like in firms of recruitment consultants and, in fairness, they are not all like this but, by basing your judgements on these assumptions, you will be forming a correct appreciation of the task you face, notably:

- **Give yourself time.** Don't try to fill in recruitment consultants' forms in a rush. Set aside an hour when you can concentrate properly on the task.

- **Rough out what you are going to say.** The best way to do this is by photocopying the blank form and using the copy for your rough. Make sure that what you want to say fits the space. Avoid having to cramp up your last few words at the end of a line. If you really make a hash of the form, ask the consultant to send you a fresh one.

- **Check your spelling!** Remember you've
  not got the spell checker helping you this
  time so, if you are uncertain about any
  words you want to use, look them up in
  the dictionary. Belt and braces, get
  someone whose spelling and grammar
  you can trust to cast an eye over your
  rough.

- **Use black ink.** The chances are that your
  form will have to be photocopied or
  faxed at some point in its life. Black ink
  will ensure that photocopies and faxes
  can be read.

- **Write neatly.** This is not just a question
  of legibility, but also the time which
  consultants and employers are prepared
  to give to deciphering candidates'
  handwriting.

- **Answer the questions you are asked.**
  Don't be vague or imprecise. For example,
  if you are asked what kind of
  opportunities you are looking for, spell
  it out graphically using job titles, salary
  ranges, business sectors etc. Keep it
  simple. Keep it concise. Don't allow any
  scope for a misunderstanding to creep in
  (accessibility).

- **Articulate the key areas of your skills
  and experience.** Key areas of your skills
  and experience are what will sell you to
  prospective employers and get you the
  kind of job you want. It follows that key
  areas need to be given prominence in any
  documentation you complete for
  recruitment consultants. Key areas are the
  subject of the next section.

- **Keep your file up to date.** Don't view
  registering with a firm of consultants as a
  one-off event. Your job may change, you

may get further qualifications, your ideas on where you see your next step in life may also change – and all changes need to be communicated to the consultants who have you on file, promptly and as they happen. The penalty for failing to communicate is a double whammy. First, because the information on file is obsolete, you won't be paired with the right kind of opportunities any more. Second and more importantly your relationship with the consultant will be put at risk. Read the case study from Annie.

CASE STUDY: ANNIE, A RECRUITMENT CONSULTANT

'This super job for an applications engineer with a major machine tool manufacturer came into the office carrying a salary tag of £25–£28k. We had a candidate on file who fitted the client's spec exactly and who, according to his registration details, was looking to improve on a current earnings figure of just over £22.5k.

Having got the client interested in the candidate the first problem we ran into was when we tried to make contact with him. He was out of the country on a job, his wife told us, and wouldn't be back for ten days. We explained the situation and she agreed to pass on a message to ask him to ring us urgently (she was expecting a telephone call from him that very evening). Two days passed and we heard nothing so we rang the candidate's wife again. Yes, she said, she had spoken to him and she was surprised that he had not been in touch. She was expecting a further call from him that evening and she would give him a reminder. Another two days went by and still no word. All this time, as you can imagine, we were doing our best to keep the client warm. The client, understandably, was starting to get restless and wanting to know what was going on.

Finally after another telephone conversation with the candidate's wife we got the number of a half-built factory in Romania where he was working and, after three failed attempts, we finally got to speak to him. Why hadn't he returned our calls? Oh, he said, he thought his wife had explained: £25–£28k didn't interest him any more because he had just been given a rise!

Needless to say, we quietly removed this gentleman's name from our files. Apart from all the running round we had to do, we had the job of having to smooth things over with our client. Naturally this episode didn't do a lot for our image and, in a highly competitive industry like recruitment, we can't afford to be messed round by people who don't tell us when their circumstances change.'

True, the candidate's conduct didn't help here, but the lessons to learn from this story are that recruitment consultants don't take kindly to having their time wasted and they don't like having their reputations damaged by people who don't communicate properly.

....

MARKETING YOURSELF EFFECTIVELY BY FOCUSING ON KEY AREAS OF YOUR SKILLS AND EXPERIENCE

If you remember what we said about why companies turn to headhunting as a preferred method of recruitment, one of the reasons we highlighted was the need to target people with specific skills and experience. Advertising, because of its very nature and its openness to all and sundry, fails to target and this is why some companies choose not to use it. Given this link between headhunting and the need to target specific attributes in candidates, what follows next is that candidates who seek to be headhunted need to bring any specific attributes they have to the fore.

Identifying key areas

In all of us there is something in what we have done or the talents we have that sets us apart from the rest of the population or puts us into a very small grouping. It is these talents and experiences that we need to be focusing on and what, in this section, we will be referring to as your 'key areas'. If the aim is to get you on the receiving end of headhunters' approaches, these key areas are what you need to be pushing. Take the example of Grace.

CASE STUDY: GRACE

Grace is a human resources (personnel) manager whose career résumé reveals that she has had a pretty wide grounding in all the main HR disciplines – selection, industrial relations, salary administration and so on – but two areas of her experience fall outside the norms for someone with her background:

- Her company has a number of overseas offshoots (typically in third world countries) and Grace has been responsible for recruiting people to work in these offshoots on long-term contracts. As a result, she is completely *au fait* with all the legal aspects of working on contracts overseas and she has been involved in developing family friendly policies for people on long-term postings.

- Her company has gone over to being a 'lean' organisation, meaning a lot of first-line management and supervisory jobs have gone. As a consequence Grace has been at the forefront of a programme of shop-floor empowerment including the introduction of unsupervised production teams in a fast-moving assembly industry environment governed by 'just-in-time' principles.

These are Grace's key areas and the point to key areas is this: if a company is on the market for a no frills human resources generalist it will probably choose to go down the advertising route. If, on the other hand, it is looking for someone with experience of introducing unsupervised team working in high volume manufacturing, (that is, a fairly scarce skill) it will be tempted to opt for headhunting. There is nothing odd or special about key areas and, unless you happen to be in the early stages of your career, you are almost bound to have one or two. Let's take a few more examples.

CASE STUDIES: KEY AREAS

Lisa, who is a credit manager and whose company has embarked on a policy of zero tolerance of late payers.

Roland, who is an accountant and who, because of his company's corporate development strategies, has been involved in a large number of acquisitions and disposals.

Gary, who is an engineer and who has taught himself to program a new generation of computer numerically controlled machine tools.

> **Aldo,** who is an environmental health specialist
> who has an Italian mother and an Arabic father
> and who can speak both languages as fluently as
> he can English.

A common mistake with key areas is to end up
with too many. If you find your list exceeds six
then the chances are that what you are
looking at are not key areas but attributes
most people in your occupational group
would be expected to have. There is a further
problem to having too many key areas: the
real ones get lost among the ones that are
border-line, meaning that, from a marketing-
of-you point of view, the messages you are
trying to feed out get the sharp edges taken off
them. What to do? If you find you have a long
list of key areas, go through them again and
strike out any that might be considered run of
the mill for someone in your profession. Be
ruthless, if you have to.

Bringing key areas into prominence

Key areas of skill and experience are not just
some stand-alone factor that you commit to
page three of your cv. The trick is making
them work for you – using them proactively to
engage the attentions of headhunters, and
this brings us back to the importance of what
goes on the files of any consultants you elect
to use. Put it this way: if a job comes into the
consultant's office that is right up your street
you want to be sure that you trigger the
retrieval systems – the file search has got to
throw out your name.

Getting your key areas to the fore in the
information consultants are holding on you
can be done in two ways:

- **in writing** – on the consultant's registration form where – though all consultants' forms are different – there will usually be a place to give your key areas prominence. Watch out for questions such as 'Is there anything in your experience that you feel we ought to draw to the attention of a prospective employer?', or 'Is there anything you would like to add to the information you have given above?', or 'Please set out here details of any experience you have had which is of special interest.'

- **orally** – at an interview (and note that the formality of registration interviews with recruitment consultants varies enormously). Here you must check for signs that the consultant interviewing you is listening to what you are saying. For a start, is he or she writing it down? If not, it might be worth saying it again with a bit more emphasis this time.

Remember when you are plugging your key areas either orally or in writing that recruitment consultants, and the people responsible for inputting information onto their databases and carrying out preliminary file searches may not be too clear about what you are trying to describe. This is more likely to happen in consultancies that are generalist in the nature of the appointments they handle (as in the case of standard all-round executive search and selection practitioners). On the other hand, specialist consultancies (e.g. ones that specialise in legal appointments) should be able to pick up on the finer points of what you are seeking to put across.

The lesson here is that unless you are pretty confident that the consultancy you are dealing with is on the same wavelength, you need to take precautions to ensure that your message is accessible, i.e. capable of being received and understood. You can do this by:

- avoiding jargon
- keeping it short and simple
- not trying to feed out too many messages at once (the importance, again, of not having too many key areas).

Though it sounds like a case of dumbing it down for the benefit of the recruitment consultants, refining the messages you feed out in this way is an aspect of what we will be referring to later in the book as 'keeping control'.

GOLDEN RULE 4

Market yourself effectively.

On the subject of experience and skills, what is also very evident is the scope that exists for extending your capacity to be headhunted by extending and building on what you have to offer. Any opportunity to add new skills or broaden your experience should therefore be grabbed with both hands.

GOLDEN RULE 5

Add to your value.

....

AVAILABILITY: MAKING SURE THAT HEADHUNTERS CAN GET HOLD OF YOU

Availability is a major issue, as these quotes from headhunters illustrate.

> 'We had a copy of this person's cv. On it she put her home telephone number and said she could be contacted after 6.00 p.m. There was also the number of a mobile. We tried ringing the home number between 6 p.m. and 6.30 p.m. three evenings on the trot only to find there was never any answer. As for the mobile, it was always switched off.'

> 'Every time we tried to contact this particular candidate, his number was engaged. In the end we gave up.'

> 'We left umpteen messages on her answering machine but she never returned any of them.'

> 'We had no telephone number for this candidate – just his home address. As it turned out, his number was ex-directory and since we already had four other suitable candidates to put forward to our client we decided we could afford to give him a miss.'

It doesn't take too much working out that you won't get headhunted if you're never there to take the headhunters' calls, but what these comments also illustrate are:

- the extent to which headhunters use the telephone (almost to the exclusion of any other form of communication)
- their impatience with people who are hard to contact (they move onto someone else).

These observations are manifestations of the fast-moving worlds professional headhunters live in – worlds in which they need to get results both for their clients and for themselves.

Make no bones about it, telephone contactability is as important to you as anything else in the business of being headhunted, and this is why we devote a little time to ensuring that you meet the criteria. Don't whatever you do dismiss availability as a minor issue – we know plenty of people who missed out on being headhunted simply because they could not be contacted on the telephone.

Where headhunters get their telephone numbers from remains a mystery to most people but there are three likely sources:

- public information, i.e. the telephone directory or the telephone company's directory enquiries service
- someone who knows you (possibly the person who gave the headhunter your name)
- your cv or other documentation stored in the headhunter's files (e.g. a recruitment consultant's registration form).

Generally, you will need to consider three possible points of telephone contact:

- your office
- your home
- your mobile phone.

We'll look at each of these in turn and see if there are any wrinkles that need to be ironed out.

Availability at work

Headhunters may choose to ring you during normal office hours in which case they will use the telephone number of your place of work. If you happen to answer the phone, then fine, but problems can arise when you are out or unable to take the call for other reasons (such as you happen to be in a meeting). The headhunter may try again, or a message to return the call may be left with a telephonist or a secretary, or, increasingly these days, on voice mail. Why so many people fail to return their telephone calls is, on the face of it, one of life's great mysteries. But, if there is a rational explanation it is this: the amount of sales cold telephone calling targeted on people in business has spiralled in recent years – so much so that the average over-burdened manager or professional person is getting very selective about which calls they return.

Unfamiliar names certainly don't clamour for attention and, since no sector is more culpable of saturation-point unsolicited telephone selling than recruitment, the chances of Mr Jones of Jones Executive Search & Selection being picked out to have his call returned could turn out to be pretty slim. So what's the answer here? Unfortunately there isn't one, except to be disciplined about returning your telephone calls, even if you find the idea painful. The penalty, remember, is some headhunter somewhere with the job of your dreams, giving up on you because you can't be contacted.

Availability at home

This is where most difficulties arise as our

headhunters' remarks at the beginning of this section testify. There are three reasons why:

- headhunters are disposed towards ringing people at home because it is usually easier for them to talk. There is not the problem of paper-thin office walls or eaves-dropping telephonists to contend with. Ringing people at home is therefore something they tend to do a lot

- most people are only at home in the evenings or at weekends – even then, only before and after certain times

- home telephones have other users, e.g. other members of the family.

The key to good home telephone availability comes under the heading of 'keeping control' which is one of our golden rules for being headhunted that comes up in the next chapter. 'Keeping control' in this instance is keeping control of when headhunters telephone you, i.e. making sure, as far as you can, that they telephone you when you are likely to be in. There are two very simple ways of doing this:

- on your cv or on any other document that is likely to find its way onto a headhunter's desk, put your normal home arrival time alongside your home telephone number, e.g. 'after 7 p.m.'

- if a headhunter rings you at work and if it is agreed between the two of you that it would be better to ring you at home later, similarly state a time.

In giving home arrival times allow yourself thirty minutes' leeway. There will be some evenings when you will be late, just as there will be some evenings when you will be early, but at least you will not be in the situation where the headhunter is ringing you several evenings consecutively and finding there is no one in (a signal to the headhunter to give up).

Carrying out an availability audit

An interesting exercise to carry out is an availability audit. Put yourself in the position of a headhunter trying to contact you at home and see what joy you have. If your cv says you are in after 7.00 p.m., see what would happen if someone tried to ring you at 7.05 p.m. each evening over a two-week period. Would you be in? Would anyone be in? Most importantly, how many times would the number be engaged?

This exercise will help you to expose flaws in your availability – flaws that will probably surprise you, for example:

- how often you are late
- how often you pick up the phone as soon as you walk through the door
- how long members of your family spend chatting and tying up the line.

The purpose of an availability audit is to throw up points for action like:

- is 7 p.m. too early? Should you be broadcasting that you arrive back home at 7.30 p.m. just to be on the safe side?

- is your telephone line busy in the evening? The causes range from teenagers talking to their friends through to someone surfing the Internet. To an incoming caller it can be very irritating indeed. If you have this problem give some thought to getting your telephone company to provide you with a call waiting signal (a bleep to tell you someone is trying to get through) or to putting in a second line.

- Answering machines? Yes, by all means use an answering machine, but do remember to check the messages the minute you walk in. (The same goes for e-mails if there is an e-mail address on your cv.)

Availability by mobile phone

In theory, mobile phones should provide the perfect answer to availability. There are two snags, however:

- signal strength: your mobile phone won't work in all areas
- sometimes you will have it switched off, e.g. in places where it could cause interference with other equipment or where it would be difficult to take calls or irritating to other people.

Inviting headhunters to call you on mobile phones, e.g. by putting a number of a mobile phone on your cv, needs to be carefully thought through. If your mobile phone is switched off for long periods, or if your normal day takes you to places where signal strength is poor, then it is probably best left off. Though headhunters will appreciate the ups and downs of mobile phone reception, their patience will start to run thin if they are greeted time and time again by 'sorry the telephone you have just called is switched off – please try later'. If you do choose to use a mobile phone as an availability aid, it is advisable to opt for a service with a message taking facility (and, do make sure to check your messages!).

Availability is a vast subject and we have only skimmed across the surface here. Part of the fun to availability is working out your own solutions – solutions that fit your work patterns and life-style.

| GOLDEN RULE 6 |

Be available.

Questions and answers

Do headhunters keep pestering you?

Q One of my big fears with headhunters is that once they've got your name, they won't leave you alone. Is this true, or am I being unnecessarily cautious?

A Headhunters come in all shapes and sizes (see the answer to the next question), but the overwhelming majority would be swift to condemn the practice of approaching candidates who have already been placed and for whom fees have been charged. This situation apart, you need to differentiate between headhunters who are trying to make an honest job of matching people to their clients' needs and those who go round peppering the people they are headhunting with anything and everything. With some justification, the latter could be described as pesterers and, in practice, they might prove hard to get rid of. Still, it would be a pity to allow your view of headhunters to be coloured by the activities of a tiny minority.

Headhunters who lack professionalism

Q Is there such a thing as a bad executive search consultant? I ask because I received an approach recently from someone who seemed to be very lacking in professional skills.

A Sadly, the answer is yes. Headhunting is a self-selecting profession and almost anyone with an office and a telephone can set up. How long they last is another matter entirely. Ultimately, it is a problem for the company commissioning the search if the headhunter falls short of the mark. What you mustn't do though is allow your view of the headhunter to colour your opinion of the company or the job.

Mixing in the right circles

Q Is it true that top headhunters only do business in exclusive West End restaurants or fashionable holiday resorts? If so, what chance do I stand?

A Not all headhunters are into champagne life-styles and, if you really want to know, most of them do the bulk of their business over the telephone. Most importantly, don't allow the popular image of headhunters to make you feel socially inferior or excluded. Headhunters like everyone else are in business to make money and they only make money by finding people like you and placing them in jobs.

How headhunters get your name

Q I am intrigued to know where a headhunter got my name from because I have never had any previous dealings with either the person or his company. I did ask him to tell me but he refused to say. Can you help to satisfy my curiosity?

A Like journalists, headhunters are notoriously cagey about revealing their sources. As to explanations there could be several, some of them are probably more mundane than you are expecting to hear:

- Have you been active on the job market recently? If you have, then your name may be on the files of a recruitment business with which the headhunter has an association.

- Unknown to you, one of your colleagues may be on the headhunter's net.

- Similarly an ex colleague or a professional contact may be on the headhunter's net.

- Are you a director of the company? If so, your name will appear in the annual report and accounts.

- Does your name appear in any other information about the company that is in the public domain? Equally has your name featured in any recent media coverage?

- Have you been looking for staff recently? If so, has your name appeared in any recruitment advertisements?

- The headhunter could have got your name by asking your company's telephonist.

TICK YOUR PROGRESS
....

✓ Don't expect to be headhunted if you are inexperienced or newly qualified.

✓ Don't expect approaches in a slump.

✓ Concentrate on your lifelong interview and

making yourself 'person perfect' and 'work perfect'.

✓ Use your contacts to establish links with proper search consultants. Play them at their own game.

✓ Be visible to people outside your own company.

✓ Use the abundance of recruitment consultants to pick and choose. Get your name on the right files.

✓ Make file search work for you by helping consultants to match you with the right opportunities.

✓ Use key areas of your skills and experience to market yourself to headhunters.

✓ Take every chance to add to your value by extending your skills and experience.

✓ Make yourself available to headhunters. Concentrate on getting your one call contactability right.

Part three

RECEIVING APPROACHES

Now you've done all that you can to get onto the headhunters' nets what happens when you pick up the phone and find yourself speaking to one?

In Part Three we look at handling approaches, in particular:

- how you should view an approach: asking yourself why the headhunter has singled you out

- the dangers of succumbing to flattery: not letting headhunters' approaches go to your head

- judging the competition: is it just you in the frame or has the headhunter got others on the list?

- who should you be telling? When to keep silent about an approach and when to be saying something to your company

- keeping control of approach

- helping headhunters understand where you are coming from.

....

REASONS WHY YOU ARE STILL NOT BEING HEADHUNTED

'I've done everything you've suggested but I'm still sitting here waiting for the telephone to ring. Have I got something wrong?'

The magic hasn't worked, but before you start jumping to too many conclusions run through the checklist on pages 25 to 27 again. In addition, ask yourself the following questions:

- How closely do you match the 'person perfect' and 'work perfect' ideal? Do you stand up to the scrutiny of the lifelong interview or are there blemishes on your track record? Be honest with yourself here. A headhunter's reputation is at stake with candidates put before a client, and if there is any doubt about any aspect of your job performance or character, he or she is not going to take the risk. If you fall into this category, don't rely over-much on being headhunted; find some other way of advancing your career (e.g. by replying to job ads).

- Are you paying sufficient attention to your networks? Are you maximising your opportunities to mix and mingle with others in your profession, e.g. by joining professional institutions, going on external courses, being active in bodies like trade associations?

- Are you maximising your opportunities to get your name in information that is in the public domain? For example, is there anything about your work that might catch the media's attention?'

- Do the right firms of recruitment consultants have you on file? Are you reviewing the performance of recruitment consultants along the lines we suggested on page 46?

- Do your cv and registration forms satisfy the 'one quick read' test? Do they aptly describe who you are and where you are coming from, i.e. are they accessible? A good clue to poor accessibility is where consultants are repeatedly phoning you about opportunities that you view as unsuitable. In some cases this will be a reflection on the consultants and their ineffectiveness but, if it keeps happening, read it that you might have a problem with your accessibility.

- Along with accessibility, are you articulating those key areas of skill and experience as you should be doing?

- Are you taking your telephone calls? Are you doing anything else to frustrate headhunters who may be trying to get through to you?

- At what level are you job seeking? Remember that proper search is very costly and companies are only likely to use it for their very senior appointments? If you are targeting the under £50k per annum bracket your chances of being headhunted will be correspondingly less than someone who is in the market for jobs higher up the ladder, i.e. it's not a reflection on you but on the recruiting methods companies prefer.

- Are people with your skills and experience in demand? If you are in a profession where the supply of people is plentiful or where good jobs are hard to come by, you will find companies can fill their vacancies by less expensive methods than search.

Still baffled? Have a little patience. Being headhunted is not an everyday event, and it is wrong to see it as such.

....

PREPARING TO TAKE THE CALLS

Your first surprise may be finding that the headhunter is someone you know. It is perfectly normal for this to happen in situations where companies are doing their own headhunting. You will be known to someone who works for the company (or someone who is close to them) and the same someone will be given the job of making contact with you. The call you take from Angela who used to work with you isn't just to natter about old times. Angela's company has got a vacancy and Angela has put your name forward. Now Angela has been volunteered to sound you out. Lesson one: be ready to jump from chat into prick up your ears and listen mode.

Where your name has been sourced from a file search the person making contact with you could be a consultant who has spoken to you previously (e.g. someone who has interviewed you at some point in the past). He or she could be one of those consultants who wears more than one hat in life: someone who does selection and search assignments. Where this happens the name of the consultant and the firm should be familiar to you.

Some approaches, however, will be from consultants and organisations that you have never heard of before, and the fact that you are being headhunted may only materialise part way through the conversation. Where names mean nothing to you, it is a pretty strong clue that you have been sourced by proper search.

In any of these situations – and for different reasons – approach is something that tends to

take you unawares. Also headhunters' prefer-
ence for using the telephone brings them into
direct voice contact with you and at moments
that won't be of your choosing.

> *'I don't have the luxury of a private office
> and so when I received a call from a
> headhunter the other day it was very difficult
> to have a conversation.'*

Most headhunters are schooled to be empa-
thetic about the work situations of the people
they are contacting. Any calls made to a
person's place of work will normally therefore
be prefaced by questions such as 'Are you free
to talk?', or 'Would it be easier for you to call
me back?'

Buying a little space for yourself

Even if no such question is inserted at the start
of a telephone conversation, the first action
for you to consider when you discover that
you are being headhunted is whether it would
be wise to buy yourself a little space. We say
this for a number of reasons:

- Unless you are a very controlled
  individual, receiving a call from a
  headhunter tends to put your mind in a
  spin. The danger is that you don't listen
  to everything that's being said and you
  miss out on something important.

- Your location may lack privacy. You may
  be inhibited as to what you are able to
  say by worries about being overheard. The
  risk again is you don't listen properly, or
  you make responses that sound guarded
  and lacking in commitment.

- The headhunter may ask questions such

as 'Are you looking to make a move?'
Because you haven't thought about it
before, you won't know what to say.

A polite exit line to these calls that come at
you out of the blue is to say that it is difficult
for you to talk just at the moment but can you
please phone back at (state a time). Just so that
you are clear on what we are saying here,
don't go cold into your first phone call with a
headhunter. First impressions could be at
stake (if the headhunter is someone you don't
know) and, unless you have received a number of approaches recently and are in the
swing of things, you will benefit from having a
few hours to prepare yourself.

By all means ask headhunters if you can
contact them in the evening at a time when
you will be in the privacy of your own four
walls. Headhunters are not nine-to-five people
and, as a rule, they will be perfectly happy to
speak with you out of hours. The only capital
sin here is failing to ring the headhunter at the
time you agreed. Waiting round for people to
phone you in the evening (meals on hold,
going out times delayed) is, needless to say,
frustrating and annoying for those on the
receiving end. Don't let your relationship with
a headhunter get off to a bad start. Don't
create the impression that future dealings with
you could be painful. Remember the importance of first impressions with people. First
impressions are the ones that stick.

Points to think through

Having bought yourself a bit of time, you can
use it to prepare for your conversation with
the headhunter.

*'How can I possibly prepare when I don't
know what the headhunter wants to talk to
me about?'*

The detail into which a headhunter will want
to go in this opening discussion will depend to
a large extent on the headhunter's individual
style. Also, a headhunter who knows you may
be quicker to get down to brass tacks than one
who has never had a conversation with you
before.

Allowing for these variations in style, it's
sensible to expect any headhunter to be seeking to establish in the very broadest terms:

- that you can do the job (confirmation
  that what he or she has been led to
  believe is correct)
- that you would be interested.

With a headhunter who knows you the
emphasis will be on the latter. The bottom
line to this interrogation is that the headhunter will want to know that talking to you
isn't a waste of time.

For you, being prepared means entering into
this dialogue with an aim. Your aim is to move
the process onto the next stage, hence you
should be prepared to give answers that convey:

- confidence in your own ability
- the impession that, though you are happy
  with your present job you would never
  rule out any move that would be
  advantageous to your career, i.e. you are
  open to offers (we will have more to say
  about never shutting the doors in
  headhunters' faces a little later in this
  chapter).

Being prepared also means having some
answers ready for questions about salary

expectations. These may or may not come up in your first discussion with the headhunter, but you should certainly have some ideas thought through about what kind of offer would tempt you out of the tree just in case you are asked. If the question 'What are you looking for?' is put to you in your first conversation with a headhunter don't mince words, but at the same time be aware that anything you say needs to be carefully considered. There are two reasons for this:

- it could send out the completely wrong signals (notably where you flag up salary expectations that are too high and which will only serve to bring the approach to a premature and unwanted close)
- it sets the benchmarks for future negotiations, i.e. starting too low can also be a mistake.

With the second you should be aware that negotiation of the package forms a significant part of approach and companies who go in for headhunting are usually open to flexibility. Read these comments along with what we have to say about negotiating the package in Part Four. Getting headhunted is a golden opportunity to drive a good bargain for yourself and, suffice is to say at this stage, the opportunity should never be missed by failing to tweak your ambitions up sufficiently.

Given these two risks any statements you make about salary expectations at these early stages should, at the same time as being realistic, express your willingness to be flexible and, if needs be, to enter into negotiation. Remember that you are talking to the headhunter here and that the headhunter will probably be your go-between in the negotiation.

If the headhunter is looking at a job that at

tops is going to pay £10k a year less than you are already earning, there won't be a great deal of point in proceeding further. However, in most approach situations there is a lot of scope for manoeuvre, hence the advisability of rolling events onto the next stage.

| **GOLDEN RULE 7** |

Be prepared.

....

HEARING HEADHUNTERS OUT

'I've got a great job with a great company and I get tired of consultants ringing me up all the time and asking me if I would be interested in such and such a position with one of their clients. I usually end up telling them where to go.'

Putting up the shutters to headhunters is never a good idea, because:

- many of the best jobs are filled by headhunting and you could be turning your back on the opportunity of a lifetime. Opportunity rarely knocks twice, as we all know
- you never know when you are going to need a headhunter. The job you are so confident about and you feel so happy in could suddenly fold for reasons that are not within your control.

For these reasons it is always in your interests to hear headhunters out – even though you may not be in the market for a job move at the precise moment they phone.

GOLDEN RULE 8

Don't close doors.

....

VIEWING APPROACH

There is a natural tendency to find approach flattering. Here at last is the proof that you have talents someone wants and the recognition that you have craved for all these years is suddenly presented to you on a plate.

Those most susceptible to feelings of flattery are:

- those who have never been headhunted before
- those who are in dead-end jobs where there is not much to be happy about
- those who are out of work.

While a moderate dose of feeling pleased with yourself because you have succeeded in being headhunted is harmless, letting it go to your head is riddled with danger. Read the experiences of Alan and Jo.

CASE STUDY: ALAN

'The boss had been giving me a hard time recently so telling him that I had received an approach gave me a great deal of satisfaction. Unfortunately it rebounded when I ended up not being offered the job.'

CASE STUDY: JO

'I allowed the feel-good I got from being head-hunted to get in the way of my better judge-ment. I took a job that was wrong for me and

now I am in an even bigger fix than I was
before.'

Staying detached and not succumbing to flattery is not made any easier by the intrigue and
excitement that approach generates, but keeping a proper perspective is important for a
number of reasons:

- it holds you back from ill-considered
  actions (like Alan's)

- it allows you to view the job under
  discussion for what it is – whether it is
  right for you or not is something you will
  be able to judge objectively

- it will keep your expectations in check so
  that your ego won't take an almighty
  blow if, for any reason, you don't get
  offered the job

- it will enable you to negotiate the best
  possible deal for yourself (someone who
  feels flattered also tends to feel grateful –
  meaning they pick up the first offer that's
  put on the table and the opportunity to
  get a really good deal is missed).

GOLDEN RULE 9

Don't be dazzled.

FINDING OUT WHAT THE HEADHUNTER HAS TO OFFER

What individual headhunters divulge in the
course of their first telephone conversation
with you will vary enormously. In some

instances you will learn little; at the other extreme, you may be given a very detailed description of the position and what's expected. You may even learn the identity of the company, and this will certainly be the case if the company is doing its own head-hunting. Is there anything fishy about head-hunters who are cagey with you in these preliminary discussions? The answer is no. The identity of the company and precise details of the job may be withheld at these early stages for a number of perfectly feasible reasons:

- the headhunter hasn't got clearance from the company either to reveal its identity or move beyond the generalities

- the company may compete with your present employer (a common occurrence with headhunting). If so, knowledge of the vacancy and its circumstances (e.g. a senior executive leaving or on the point of dismissal) could have some commercial advantage. In these cases the company won't want to reveal its identity or any confidential information until the candidate has indicated a serious interest in the position or has got past some of the preliminary selection hurdles

- irrespective of competition, the company may view the appointment as confidential for other reasons (e.g. share price sensitivity)

- the company may be doing a fishing exercise, i.e. getting the headhunter to come up with names before making a decision on whether to proceed with the appointment or not.

Attending interviews with headhunters

Some headhunters will prefer to have these preliminary discussions with you eyeball to eyeball. This could be because of:

- a reluctance to go into anything confidential over the phone
- a desire to take a look at you, i.e. as part of a selection process.

You will find on the whole that headhunters can be quite accommodating when it comes to fitting in meetings out of hours. They appreciate that getting away from work isn't always easy, particularly at short notice. Where you could run into a problem, however, is with a headhunter who isn't based locally and who may have to fit you in with other meetings as part of a business trip.

The advice here is don't be difficult with a headhunter who is trying to get to see you. Don't be like one candidate we know and say that you are only available on Sundays.

Choice of venue for these preliminary meetings with headhunters is worth dwelling on for a few moments. The choice is normally:

- the headhunter's offices
- on neutral ground such as a hotel or dedicated conference suite.

CASE STUDY: IAN

'A headhunter arranged to meet me at a hotel close to one of the motorway junctions which has its own conference centre. Imagine my shock when I bumped into our sales director in the car park. It transpired that he had been interviewing candidates for a sales position. Naturally he wanted to know what I was doing there.'

For reasons best illustrated by Ian's embarrassing experience, selecting hotels that are popular business venues isn't a good idea for meetings with headhunters. The same goes for headhunters' offices that are in busy city thoroughfares where there is a chance that you will be seen. (Let's face it, entering a headhunters' offices is a straight give away as to what you are up to.) If you can sway it, arrange to meet the headhunter at an out of town location, e.g. small country hotel.

Listening to headhunters

The most important action you need to take when a headhunter is outlining a position to you is to switch on your ears.

Jo (in the case study on page 86) is an example of someone who was too consumed with the euphoria of the occasion to take in all that was being said to her. Instead, she listened selectively, hearing to a large extent what she wanted to hear.

These preliminary briefings by headhunters are important because they are the point at which you will be taken from knowing absolutely nothing about the job onto your first level of appreciation. Some things will be said that will never be repeated again and a lot of the very basic information about both the job and the company will be imparted at this stage (even though the name of the company may still be withheld).

GOLDEN RULE 10

Listen.

FINDING OUT WHERE YOU STAND

'I made the mistake of assuming that being headhunted meant the job was mine'.

Finding out where you stand is important because it will determine to a large extent how you handle an approach. Where you stand will normally be in one of three broad categories:

- **the single runner in a one-horse race** – this is most likely where companies are doing their own headhunting: where you are known to the company either directly or through an intermediary and where you are being approached because you have some skill/experience the company wishes to acquire. The company's knowledge of you also has a comfort factor for them.

- **one of a very select bunch** – a shortlist of candidates who will be well researched and matched to the client company's needs, i.e. the typical outcome of proper search. Again the comfort factors rank high

- **one of many** – in most instances this will be because you are in the trawl from a file search or a number of file searches (companies frequently go to more than one recruitment consultant). Speed is the essence of the decision to go down this recruitment route and matching of candidates to clients' specifications will not have been carried out to any consistent or exacting standard. Comfort factors are fairly low on the agenda.

Suitability will be determined by the selection process that is still in front of you.

The point to listing these categories is to illustrate the wide variations in where you could be standing when you receive an approach. At one extreme, with no competition and big comfort factors at the back of you, you will have to slip up pretty badly not to get the job. At the other end of the scale (i.e. one of many) your position is only slightly up on someone who has written in response to an advertisement. Your chances of eventually getting the job are relatively slight.

This range of possible situations is yet another reason for not letting the approach go to your head.

What would be useful for you to know, of course, is which of these categories you fall into. Armed with this information, you will be able to gauge how best to proceed.

Asking headhunters outright to tell you how they got your name could be viewed by some as asking them to disclose a trade secret. Some may oblige but, as the experience of one of our questioners at the end of Part Two bears out, others may be less forthcoming. Fortunately, however, there are usually a few clues scattered about:

- Is the headhunter known to you? If so, there is a good chance you are the single runner in a one-horse race. (Feel excited now.)

- Is the headhunter from outside the recruitment industry, i.e. not a consultant? Again there is a good chance you are a single runner. (Still feel excited.)

- Is the headhunter a consultant who works

for a firm you have had dealings with in the past, e.g. job applications? If the answer is yes, the likelihood is that you have been pulled out of a file search. You are probably in the 'one of many' category. (Get those expectations down.)

- Is the name of the headhunter's firm not one that you immediately recognise? Does it have a swish address, e.g. West End? This sounds like proper search meaning you will be 'one of a very select bunch'. (Allow your expectations to drift back up again.)

- Listen for the coded language. 'Your name has been suggested to us ...' 'You have been brought to our notice ...' suggests proper search. On the other hand 'We have read your details/seen a copy of your cv ...' has the ring of a file search (react accordingly).

GOLDEN RULE 11

Find out where you stand.

One of the points to knowing where you stand is that it should help to give you an idea of what selection hurdles you still face:

- what lies between you and getting the job
- how tough it is going to be
- how your chances rate.

Companies doing their own headhunting

With the strong possibility that you are the single runner in the race, it is reasonable to expect a fairly minimal and informal selection process. The company knows you and your work so you have already satisfied the lifelong interview test. What else is left to talk about? Discussion will probably centre around the finer points. How do you feel about the job they have in mind? How do they view you as one of their team?

There will be meetings that won't seem like interviews and it is unlikely that you will be subjected to any form of selection test. Pretty soon both parties are going to know whether this is a marriage made in heaven or a complete and utter mismatch. Either the job offer is put in your hands or you part good friends.

Proper search

Here the probability is that the headhunter has never met you before. Your name has been recommended but the headhunter will still need to put the stamp of approval on you before passing you onto his or her client. Stand by, therefore, for full blown, in-depth interviews and the very latest in psychological tests. Though you won't be up against a lot of competition, there is still plenty of scope for failing to come up to scratch.

File search

A lot will depend on precisely what the recruitment consultant has been commissioned to do. In many cases it will just be the file search and it will be over to the company to carry out the selection process. Sometimes recruitment consultants will be asked to provide expertise (e.g. interviewing, administering selection tests) but it is reasonable to expect their input to be minimal. The selection process you will face will be whatever the company determines as appropriate. In this, it will probably be identical to the process to which candidates sourced by advertising are subjected.

Warning: What all of these situations have in common is that at the point of approach you are *not* being offered the job. Obvious though this may sound, plenty of people fall into the trap of making mistaken assumptions, as Chhaya in the case study below did.

CASE STUDY: CHHAYA

'I work in the water treatment industry and this was the first time that I had been headhunted. The phone rang one day and there was a smooth-sounding character on the other end of the line who asked me if I would be interested in running a new joint venture company that his client was setting up in partnership with an American firm.

'I had been feeling in a rut for sometime so I viewed this telephone call as very timely from my point of view. With no hesitation at all, therefore, I accepted the headhunter's invitation to come and see him at the offices of his firm.

'I must say that I was very impressed with the headhunter when I met him – his office set-up, the cut of his clothes, the way he exuded confidence – here to me was a successful guy with whom I was pleased to be associated. How did he get my name? He smiled and said he had a number of contacts in the water treatment industry and several of these had suggested that I would be an ideal match for his client's needs. He then proceeded to expand on the job and the envisaged package and everything I heard was magic to my ears. At this point, he revealed his client's identity and, since they happened to be one of the leading names in the industry, any lingering doubts I had immediately disappeared. We parted on an upbeat note with the head-hunter saying he would set up an early meeting with his client's managing director and get back to me within the next few days.

'In hindsight I suppose it was naive of me to take it that the job was mine, but I did and on the strength of this belief, I cracked a bottle of champagne at home that night. Next day I went to see my boss. I told him I had received the offer I couldn't refuse and that my letter of notice would be in the internal post.

'The coin didn't drop until the next meeting – the one with the managing director of the headhunter's client. The conversation this time was punctuated with 'possibles' and 'what ifs' then finally it emerged that there were two other candidates in the frame. The upshot was I didn't get the job; in fact it finished up with the American partner in the joint venture bringing over one of their own people. Fortunately my boss was understanding when I asked to with-draw my notice, but it really was a case of having to eat humble pie.'

What we are seeing here is:

- someone with no previous experience of being headhunted
- the feeling of flattery at work
- a headhunter who is too intent on 'selling the job'.

GOLDEN RULE 12

Don't confuse approaches with job offers.

....

MOVING THE APPROACH FORWARD

To sum up, you are now at the point where you have:

- prepared yourself
- detached yourself from any feelings of flattery
- listened to what the headhunter has got to say
- found out where you stand and gauged the extent and quality of the competition you are up against.

Sooner or later in your first discussion with the headhunter he or she will be seeking to establish your level of interest in the job and this is where we go back to your preparation. There is always the possibility of course that the headhunter has read you wrongly. The job is way off target (career wise or pay wise) and carrying on discussions any further is pointless. Here your task is to disengage from the headhunter without creating the impression that you are:

- a time waster
- difficult/awkward/impossible to please
- one of those candidates who don't know what they want (candidates who recruitment specialists dread).

Later on we will be looking at the importance of keeping your relationships with headhunters sweet. Needless to say, the point at which you say 'sorry, not interested', is a critical one and we will be devoting some space to helping you get this right – or as right as you can.

Assuming, however, that the opportunity

the headhunter has described to you is of
interest, you will be seeking to move the
approach forward to the next stage. As we
have seen, the next stage will depend on
where you stand. It could mean, for instance,
interviews with the headhunter (possibly
coupled with selection tests) or it could mean
your details being passed over to the client.

Control

Control is an important part of moving
approach forward. Control allows for the following:

- Approach follows a different path to
  companies' normal selection procedures.
  Some parts are left out, others are leap-
  frogged, while consultants fill in for
  executives of the company at critical
  points.

- Some companies may not be familiar with
  approach. Some may be first time users.

- Consultants may not be familiar with the
  companies. Their knowledge of the
  companies who are their clients may not
  be very complete.

- Consultants may not be very proficient,
  e.g. not very proficient in interviewing
  skills.

- Consultants may be too focused on their
  commissions. Under this heading come
  consultants who try to sell jobs to
  candidates.

GOLDEN RULE 13

Keep control.

Making sure headhunters know where you are coming from

Your first piece of keeping control as the selection process moves on is to ensure that the headhunter understands you. Bearing in mind that you may not have been put through a formal selection interview, an early task is for you to set out your stall.

GOLDEN RULE 14

Set out your stall.

There are two objectives to setting out your stall:

- headhunters need to understand you because at this stage, they will have a better appreciation than you of the job and the company. If they understand where you are coming from they will be better placed to pick up a mismatch

- approach provides you with an opportunity to negotiate a good deal for yourself. Setting your stall out is the start to negotiation.

Setting out your stall includes:

- describing what you do at the moment (the full range of your responsibilities)

- the details of your package (pay, bonuses, type of car plus any other significant perks such as share options and an estimation of their worth)

- how you see your career developing and the kind of things you would be seeking to achieve if you moved to another job

- anything you see as a potential obstacle to you in moving companies, e.g. a long

period of notice or a restraint clause
dictating which areas and industries you
are able to work in

- any special needs, e.g. needs dictated by
health problems or disabilities.

A quick flick through this list will show that in
most cases this is the kind of information that
would be set out on a job application form or
elicited at a preliminary interview. In approach
situations, application forms are often not
completed until well into the selection process
or they are overlooked altogether (the latter
being most common where companies are
doing their own headhunting without the
benefit of professional expertise and support).
There may not even be a preliminary interview, or it could be just reduced to an informal
chat.

Failing to set out your stall invites the danger
of the approach proceeding on a misreading
meaning you could be well into the selection
process before you discover that the job is not
what you are looking for or the company
discovers that you are subject to a contractual
restraint that is not to their liking. Everyone
will feel that their time has been wasted and,
perversely perhaps, it could prove hard for you
to get your relationship with the headhunter
back on track.

An even bigger danger of course is you
ending up in a job that is completely wrong
for you.

Warning: In setting out your stall don't fall
into the trap of trying to make it fit the job the
headhunter has just described to you. If it
does, fine, but if you find yourself doing a
bending and moulding act stop in your tracks

because you are undermining any possible good that could come from the exercise.

....

AFTER THE APPROACH

If you have just received an approach from a headhunter and if the job is the job of your dreams it will be hard to suppress a feeling of excitement. OK, so you have taken on board that you've still got to go the distance with interviews, selection tests etc. and perhaps there is formidable competition left for you to beat, but it's been a good day for you all the same and you will feel a natural inclination to want to share it with someone.

Keeping approaches to yourself

Telling your nearest and dearest that you're being headhunted within the privacy of your own four walls is harmless enough, but trouble is on the agenda from the moment you start confiding in colleagues. Approach has been around for a number of years but it is still novel enough to be a talking point, meaning there is a risk always of gossip reaching the wrong ears. Dev's tale illustrates the dangers.

CASE STUDY: DEV

'Eighteen months ago I was put in charge of one of our trading divisions. This meant a good promotion for me and a big increase in my salary. Soon after I started in my new job I spotted that the division was missing out on good sales opportunities with excellent profit margins simply because we lacked manufacturing capacity. I put a case forward for major capital expenditure and steered this through the board, mainly thanks to the support I got from the managing director.

'The extensions to the plant and the creation of nearly a hundred new jobs led to quite a bit of media interest including a slot on the local TV news. To my mind it was no coincidence that shortly after this coverage I received a telephone call from a headhunter. Taking the view that you should always listen to these people, I accepted his invitation to go along to a meeting at a local hotel. What he had to say in fact turned out to be quite interesting. His client, an Australian company, was looking to set up a UK subsidiary on a greenfield site nearby and they wanted someone to run it. The salary on offer was almost twice my current earnings and a bonus was going to be thrown in once the operation moved into profit. Was I interested? I didn't know what to say and ended up telling the headhunter I would think it over.

'The mistake I made was dropping the fact that I had been headhunted to a couple of my colleagues and I suspect that it was one of these who put it in the ear of the MD. As a result the MD called me into his office and gave me a terrible roasting about loyalty and lack of commitment. How would the board see it, he asked, if I left halfway through the project I had initiated? How would it look for him after backing me? I protested that I hadn't asked to be headhunted, but he took the view that I should have informed him the minute the headhunter approached me. Worse was to come because he demanded to know there and then whether I intended to stay with the company or not. Realising, apart from anything else, that I had only had a preliminary meeting with the headhunter and that there was no guarantee I was going to get the job with the Australians I opted for saying I would stay. I rang the headhunter later the same afternoon and pulled out. To this day the MD is still being frosty with me. It could be a coincidence but the rise I got at the end of the year was way below my expectations.'

Poor Dev, he seems to have lost out both ways but the object to this case study is to illustrate how leaks of this kind can force decisions on you at the wrong time. The decision to stay or go should have been taken if and when the Australians made Dev an offer. If they didn't, then the approach from the headhunter would have stayed a secret forever and Dev's relationship with his MD would have been unimpaired.

GOLDEN RULE 15

Keep it to yourself.

Approaches from competitors

There is one important exception to the golden rule of keeping it to yourself, and one we will illustrate with Delia.

CASE STUDY: DELIA

'I am a temp controller and, up until recently, I worked for a large employment agency dealing with temporary office staff. By virtue of my position, I had full knowledge of all the agency's customers, together with our pricing policy and the profit margins to which we operate – in other words, sensitive information that would be very valuable to any of our competitors.

'One afternoon I received a telephone call from Ann who had been my boss up to two years

previously when she left to start her own business. Ann wanted to meet me for a drink and I
agreed to see her after work the following
evening.

'It turned out that Ann was doing well and
looking to expand, which was no big surprise to
me because she had taken a number of our
leading accounts with her when she left. Ann
was still waiting to hear whether the bank would
raise her overdraft but, in the meantime, she
wanted to sound me out on whether I would be
willing to go in with her as a partner. With an
expanded operation she needed more senior
management people she could rely on, she
explained.

'Though I have always had a high regard for
Ann, the idea of going into business with her was
a completely different kettle of fish. I stalled and
at the end of our conversation it was left that
Ann would contact me again when she heard
from her bank. It was true to say, however, that I
had already decided that my answer would be
no.

'Two days later the managing director called
me into her office and wanted to know what I'd
been doing taking hospitality from Ann. Though
I protested my innocence, the upshot was I got
the sack and I am now working as a temp myself.
As to Ann, her bank is still asking her to provide
more financial information, so she is starting to
have doubts that her expansion programme will
ever get off the ground.'

Extreme, yes, but Delia's experience serves to
illustrate the danger that being headhunted
can present to people who work in fiercely
competitive industries (such as temporary
office staff). Did Delia inadvertently let the cat
out of the bag by careless chatter or did
someone see her having a drink with Ann?
Whatever the source of the leak, the loss of

business to Ann undoubtedly juxtaposed in the MD's mind with Delia's access to confidential information, hence the decision to sack her was taken to protect the business. (Benefit of the doubt rarely comes into it when survival of a business is at stake.)

What should you do if you work in a highly competitive industry and you find yourself on the receiving end of an approach from a competitor?

First you must appraise the risk. Risk, as we all know, has two sides – an upside and a downside. The upside on this occasion is the job: is it a good job (the opportunity of a lifetime), or does it fall short in some way? Is it a certainty or is it subject to conditions being met? Conditions could include items such as:

- approval of more senior management, i.e. further interviews
- medicals, references etc.
- the continuation of certain trading conditions or the acceptance of an order
- as in Delia's case, the provision of funding.

The downside is what could happen to you if your company discovered that you had been cosying up to the competition. What's their past record in such situations? Do they sack people they catch red-handed, or is punishment usually commuted to a warning?

Along with the upside and downside is your ability to take the risks. Are you footloose and fancy free with few financial commitments or are you a breadwinner who needs to play it safe?

In Delia's case, she was lukewarm to Ann's proposal and unlikely to accept the job even if it was offered to her – in other words, there was little or no upside and the most sensible course of action would have been to inform her MD of Ann's approach immediately. Had she done so, it would not have appeared sinister to the MD when she heard that Delia had been seen in Ann's company.

....

KEEPING ON GOOD TERMS WITH HEADHUNTERS

In the next chapter we will be saying more about the need to keep a good relationship going with headhunters. There are two main reasons why you should be wanting to do this:

- You don't want being headhunted to end up as a one-off experience. You want the flow of approaches to keep coming.
- Headhunters can be very useful to you. They can be founts of information on companies (helpful to you as the selection process moves on) and they can play a valuable part when it comes to striking the right deal.

Having said this, it is quite evident there is a critical moment in your relationship with the headhunter: the moment when you decide for one reason or another, that you are not interested in what the headhunter has put on the table.

To put 'critical' into context, remember the following factors:

- for a company doing their own headhunting (for whom you may be the only candidate under consideration) the failure of the approach is going to mean they are left empty handed and having to go back to the drawing board. In such circumstances the likelihood is they will either shelve their plans or resort to another method of recruitment, e.g. file search or advertising. With either of these they won't have the comfort factor of a candidate they know.

- A headhunter working on a 'no placement, no fee' basis (as is quite common with file search) will be making nothing out of the time that has been spent on you.

- A consultant carrying out a proper search assignment will have put considerable time and effort into sourcing you and, though his or her fee may not be entirely dependent on placement, a failed approach is still a depressing and unwelcome outcome.

Saying no to approaches

Because of these factors, there is a risk for candidates who pull out, and the risk is that headhunters will view them from here on as difficult people who are impossible to please. Headhunters who end up feeling this way about candidates don't generally come back. Once bitten, they shy away.

Before saying no to any approach first of all apply the *negotiability test*. You do this by identifying what it is about the job that's putting you off and then seeing whether it is something that could be negotiable. We'll look at two examples.

CASE STUDY: ALLY

Ally has received an approach about a job that seems to offer good opportunities including the opportunity to work overseas, which is something she would very much like to do. The trouble is the pay is about £5k down on the figure she is looking for.

A lot of headhunted candidates put in a position like this would simply say 'sorry, not interested'. The alternative is to put the spotlight on the problem and explore further – 'The job sounds great but the salary would need an improvement. How do you rate the chances of getting your client to go up another £5k?' Again this is a classic piece of setting the agenda and keeping control – and by identifying the solution to the problem it prevents a picture forming of someone who is impossible to please. Not only is the relationship with the headhunter kept sweet but the door to negotiation is opened up also.

CASE STUDY: CLIFF

Cliff has been headhunted on behalf of a company he has no time for. The job has the appearance of a good opportunity but the company has a reputation for poor treatment of its senior staff.

There is nothing to negotiate in this situation. Cliff doesn't want the job on any terms and that is that – but the alternative to just shutting the door in the headhunter's face is to give a little time to explaining where the difficulty lies. The fact that the company doesn't project a good image in the employment market may not be known to the headhunter (this is particularly the case where headhunters are not based in the local area). The main point to get across is that the same job with a different company would be very interesting to Cliff, i.e. it is more than possible to please him.

It goes without saying that the sooner you

raise a potential area of difficulty with a headhunter, the better. For example, to find out at the end of a long and difficult negotiation about salary that you still have misgivings but on a completely different and hitherto unmentioned score is really asking for trouble.

Questions and answers

Approaches that are not genuine

Q I have heard that companies sometimes pay consultants to headhunt people they wish to get rid of. Is this true? If so, how do I know when an approach is genuine?

A The practice you are referring to is sometimes called 'headshunting', and yes, it does go on though a lot of the tales are apocryphal. How do you pick it out from a genuine approach? The answer is you can't (not if the headshunt consultants are doing their job properly) but the chances of it happening to you are so remote you can probably discount them.

At desperation point

Q I have never received an approach and I am despairing that I ever will. Meanwhile my job situation is getting intolerable. What I would like to know is whether there are any desperate measures I can take to bring myself to the attention of headhunters urgently?

A It sounds like you are relying on approach alone to get you out of a job crisis. If this is the case – stop. Approach works for some people but not for others, and to rely on it is a mistake. If you need to make a move quickly then you will do far better by answering

advertisements and tapping into your professional networks, i.e. headhunting in reverse.

Going back to ex-employers

Q Most approaches I've received from companies doing their own headhunting are from
companies I've worked for previously. I've
always taken the view that it's best to avoid
going back to former employers, but is this
sensible?

A There's no definitive answer to your question except to say:

- it depends on the company
- do not rule out anything that could play
  to your advantage.

Receiving approaches from competitors

Q I work in a highly competitive yet special-
ised industry and, if you take out poaching by
competitors, it renders my job prospects as
practically non-existent. Hopefully this
explains why I was disturbed to hear what you
had to say about telling your company the
minute you receive an approach from a competitor. Surely the best way to head off a
situation like Delia found herself in would be
to do as I always do and make sure that any
meetings with competitors are held in places
where there is no chance of being seen.

A As you quite rightly say, industries like
yours are notoriously incestuous: everyone
knows everyone else and people advance their
careers by moving from one company to the
next. Also there are usually a few old enmities
hanging round in the background so the
chance to plunge the knife in someone's back
is rarely missed. We take your point about

avoiding popular watering holes, but the fact that A is trying to poach B from C has a habit of coming out in a variety of other ways. What you must never do is assume you are safe in these situations and so do the little assessment of risks along the lines we suggest. If there is something good to go for then the risk might be worth taking. The mistake is to feel there is no risk because you have taken precautions that you believe to be foolproof.

TICK YOUR PROGRESS

- ✓ Speak to headhunters only when you're ready. Think through your situation before you get locked into conversations.

- ✓ Listen to what headhunters have to say. Don't turn your back on the opportunity of a lifetime because you don't happen to be looking for another job when the headhunter rings you.

- ✓ Keep the approaches coming. View it as good that you are being presented with an on-going picture of what's available on the market.

- ✓ Don't attach any special significance to a job simply because it's been brought to your notice by approach. Apply your normal selection criteria to deciding which jobs you go for and which jobs you leave alone.

- ✓ With approach everything you are going to learn about the job is going to be presented to you orally. It is important therefore that you listen very carefully to everything that is said.

- ✓ Finding out how the headhunter got your name and what competition you are up against will tell you how to handle the approach and what to expect next.

✓ Just because you've been approached, don't assume you've got the job. Wait for the offer in writing to be put in your hands.

✓ Keep your approaches under control. Spot the potential problems and take positive steps to avoid them. Don't rely on headhunters to do this for you.

✓ Keep your approaches to yourself. Don't tell colleagues.

✓ Judge where an approach from a competitor poses a threat to you. Weigh up the risks.

✓ Encourage headhunters to want to continue their relationship with you. Don't do anything to put them off.

Part four

NEGOTIATING THE BEST DEAL FOR YOU

Getting headhunted offers one of the best chances you will ever have to negotiate a really good package for yourself. But what do you need to do to take full advantage of this chance? How should you proceed and what factors do you need to be taking into account?

In Part Four we will look at:

- assessing your bargaining strength: how far companies will go to get your skills and experience on board

- examining job offers – knowing when to say yes, when to say no, and when to ask for more

- how headhunters can help you to secure a good deal

- enticement – how to deal with the offer you think you can't refuse

- risk: seeing where the job might not work out for you and writing in some soft landings.

SEEING TO IT THAT YOU DON'T LET THE CHANCE GO BY

Unless you are the possessor of some very sought-after skills, getting headhunted is not something that is going to happen to you regularly. Indeed, some people will never be headhunted, reflecting not any failing on their part but the relative infrequency with which approach is used and its virtual absence from some sectors of the job market. Pity, therefore, the number of people who pass up the chance of getting headhunted for no reason other than their own indecision. Take the case of Alec.

CASE STUDY: ALEC

'I received an approach about twelve months ago to take over the managing directorship of a medium sized plc. The challenge was a significant one for me as previously I had only held responsibility for the running of wholly owned subsidiaries. Unfortunately the timing of the approach was bad. The job may have been just what I wanted but I had a number of other things going on in my life at the time, hence I didn't feel that I wanted to be faced with any more major personal upheaval. I decided therefore to ask the headhunter to count me out this time round, but to keep me on file because I definitely wanted to make a move like this.'

We hope that Alec never lives to rue the day that he passed up his chance. We hope too that another good opportunity comes his way soon. The capital sin he is committing, of course, is to try to dictate terms to the market: he wants the top job running a public company but he wants it at a time to suit him. Needless to say, the market doesn't work this way. The ideal jobs don't come up to suit your time scales and, if you want to take full advantage of opportunities offered to you by approach, you need to be in a constant state of readiness to make big decisions. Unlike applying for jobs you see advertised in the papers where you determine when you are active on the market and when you are not, approach arrives at any time. It doesn't conform to nice tidy patterns and you should never expect it to.

Another point of interest in Alec's case is the way he sought to rationalise his indecision. No one likes to think of themselves as indecisive so rationalisations such as 'too much going on in my life' are put up as the excuse for what is really no more than a plain bit of shilly-shallying. Remember: next time you hear yourself rationalising indecision, pull yourself up in your tracks.

GOLDEN RULE 16

Don't look gift horses in the mouth.

....

ASSESSING YOUR BARGAINING STRENGTH

How far will companies be prepared to go to have your skills and talents on board? In approach situations, what power do you have to your elbow to tweak a really good deal for yourself?

Bargaining strength needs to be considered under four headings:

- the reason why you have been singled out for the approach
- competition
- the company's flexibility and willingness to negotiate
- the level of pain that will be inflicted on the company if the approach fails.

Each of these has a bearing on the extent to which companies will be willing to dig deeper into their pockets.

Reasons for the approach

There are four likely reasons why you have
been singled out as a target for approach:

- you've got talents, skills and experience
  the company is keen to acquire
- you can bring knowledge to the company
  that will give it some commercial
  advantage
- the company feels comfortable with you
  because they know you
- you offer a quick solution.

Your bargaining strength in approach situations – your ability to test the company's
flexibility – depends first and foremost on
which of these categories you fit into. For
example, a company will fork out more if it
feels you have skills and talents it sorely needs.
On the other hand, it will be less inclined
towards largesse if all you offer is a short-cut.

Competition

It is a simple economic fact of life that,
irrespective of what it is you have to offer, the
scarcer it is (or appears to be) the higher the
price it will fetch. In recruitment terms this
puts people who are choices of one in the
optimum position of strength. Conversely
people who are seen as one of many will find
it hard to flex their bargaining muscles. Where
they do, they run the risk of being passed by.
The company will offer the job to someone
else who is less demanding.

Flexibility and willingness to negotiate

As a rule, companies go into headhunting prepared to do some tweaking of the package to attract the right people. Where they start hesitating is where the tweaking might give them problems with their internal pay and perks relativities – for example, peer groups up in arms because they see newcomers arriving on higher salaries, or seniors disaffected by erosion of their differentials. Some companies might be swayed by such concerns (tweak no further) whereas others (e.g. those cast in a more robust cultural mould or those driven by overriding considerations, such as chronic skills shortages) might carry on regardless. Relativities are less of an issue at the top where comparators are fewer, hence the often greater willingness of companies to negotiate top pay and perks packages.

Pain

The pain here is the pain that will descend on the company if, for any reason, the approach fails. Failure has a cost both in terms of the cash lavished on consultants' fees and on the consequences of the company finding itself back at square one.

Bargaining with different types of headhunters

We'll look now at the three types of head-hunting and see what bargaining strengths you can read into each situation.

Proper search

If you have been targeted by proper search consultants you can safely say that your skills and experience are hotly in demand as far as the company behind the approach is concerned. What's more, the use of proper search points to a senior position where conflict with internal relativities is unlikely to be an obstacle in the way of negotiation. Competition? Yes, there may be others in the frame apart from you, but they will be measurable in ones and twos rather than dozens. Also, with a senior job the emphasis will be on making the right selection decision. Tidying up the package to make it more attractive to one or other of the candidates will be seen as a secondary and minor consideration.

As to pain, the failure of a proper search assignment will leave the company with the lion's share of the consultant's bill to pay and the prospect of having to re-embark on a further long and costly recruiting exercise – and a senior job standing vacant at the same time. The verdict is: your bargaining strength in proper search/top job situations is considerable – go for it.

Companies doing their own headhunting

Here, even though your skills and experience will be sought after, your real bargaining strength lies in the comfort that the company's knowledge of you brings. In having this comfort factor you will probably be unique and failure of the approach means the company will have to look at recruiting routes that offer little or nothing in the way of comfort. So, even though there will be no consultants' bills to write off, the company will still experience quite a lot of pain if it finds it can't agree terms with you. In exercising your bargaining strength with companies who take a DIY approach to headhunting, the main area for you to test is their flexibility. Again the seniority of the job will be an important factor.

File search

As we have seen, one of the main reasons why companies go in for file search is quickness, meaning that your skills/experience/knowledge may not carry any great premium. What's more, with file search, competition may be substantial (the product of more than one file search) and pain for the company in the event of the file search failing will be minimal. For a start, they have made no outlay and, at the cost of a couple of days' lost time, all they have to do to get their recruiting back on track is call up a few more file searches, i.e. approach some other firms of consultants.

There is always the chance that a file search will connect you with a company that does place great worth on your bank of skills, experience and knowledge. But, other than this, view file search as a situation where your bargaining strength is low. Don't push your luck.

....

OPENING THE NEGOTIATION

Not negotiating where your bargaining power is weak

Clearly you can make a big mistake by trying to exercise bargaining strength in situations where you don't have any. Take the example of Company Y.

CASE STUDY: COMPANY Y

Company Y is trying to recruit a management accountant and a firm of recruitment consultants specialising in accountancy appointments has put forward four equally suitable candidates: Matthew, Mark, Luke and John. Matthew, Mark and Luke all seem broadly happy with the £35k figure that the consultant has bounced off them, but John is indicating he would need £40k to tempt him out of his present job. £40k would be a problem to Company Y because it is more than they pay their most senior existing accountant. They decide therefore to give John a miss and proceed to the final interview stage with Matthew, Mark and Luke. John, in fact would have been very happy to accept £35k. All he was trying to do was exercise his bargaining strength. Now he realises his mistake.

John's mistakes were, in fact, twofold:

- he tried to exercise bargaining strength where he didn't have any
- he failed to signal his flexibility (or, if he did, his signal wasn't strong enough).

The lesson to be learned from this example is to go back to what you have found out about where you stand (Golden Rule 11, page 93) and to apply the tests of bargaining strength to your situation *before* you embark on negotiating a package with a company that is trying to headhunt you. Ask yourself:

- Do they have a desperate need for your talents?
- Do they stand to gain in business terms from your knowledge and contacts?

- Does their knowledge of you offer them any comfort factors?
- Do they have freedom to negotiate with you?
- Are you unique in what you have to offer?
- Will the company be faced with a lot of pain if the approach fails?

The more ticks you can put alongside these questions, the clearer the signals will be for you to start putting up your asking price. But never neglect to leave out your flexibility and willingness to negotiate. These, if you like, are your failsafe devices just in case you have weighed the situation up wrongly.

What if you conclude that your bargaining power is weak? Almost by definition, this will be in situations where the approach has been generated by file search (where you are one of a number of faces in the frame and where your talents may not be held in any special esteem). Treat these situations rather like any other application you make, that is forget the fact that it began with an approach. Be ready though to revise your opinions because, as selection moves on and poorly matched candidates are discarded, companies will find their fields of choice dramatically reduced. Also, it could emerge that you have an attribute that the company highly prizes.

Bouncing your ideas off the headhunter

Back to negotiating. In approach situations what is often overlooked is the part that headhunters can play in you getting a good deal but, before looking at this, let's remind ourselves that there are different kinds of headhunter who, when it comes to talking to you about pay and perks, will be approaching the subject from rather different angles.

Proper search consultants

Expect proper search consultants to be giving their clients a fair amount of input on what kind of package they will need to put together to attract the right calibre of candidate to the job. Expect them, too, to play a big part in brokering the marriage: to iron out any problems and seek ways of bringing candidates and clients into states of harmony. Bear in mind here that we are moving in a world where the headhunters themselves earn big commissions and where truly astronomical figures are discussed without a blink of the eyelids. 'Being too greedy' or 'going over the top' has little or no meaning in this world, and the biggest risk you run is under-stating yourself. A tale from one proper search consultant serves as a sobering reminder.

CASE STUDY: STEPHAN

'Everything was great as far as this candidate was concerned until he started talking about his salary aspirations. As far as we could see, what he was asking for represented little advance on his current earnings package and it set us off wondering whether he was sufficiently ambitious for himself after all. Also, did his willingness to go practically sideways in salary terms illustrate that he was desperate to make the move and, if so, why?'

Another facet of proper search consultants you shouldn't miss out on is that, as a matter of self-interest, they will be keen to put the relationship with you on a strong footing. For a start the fact that they deal almost exclusively with top jobs means that though you may be a candidate today, tomorrow you could be a top job holder (possibly *the* top job holder) with one of their clients (the prospect of future billings beckons!). Even if you are not successful, then there is still the possibility of placing you somewhere else. What's more, proper search consultants never miss the chance to add another name onto their nets. This genuine desire to move into the future with you is a strength you should play on.

Company headhunters

As we have seen, company headhunters will either be executives of the company seeking to employ you or they will be figures who are 'close'. In most cases they will have been cast in the role of headhunter simply because they know you – meaning, also, they will have played some part in bringing your face into the frame.

One potential drawback with company headhunters, however, is that they may not be empowered to talk to you about the package. Because pay and perks is such a sensitive subject, some companies doing their own headhunting may prefer to keep the discussions to one-on-ones between seniors – conversations from which the person who made the original approach to you may be excluded. These situations apart, the company headhunter could be a helpful person to start off the negotiations with, but do beware the kind of company headhunter who is an interested party with an axe to grind.

CASE STUDY: KAREN

'The MD asked me if I could think of anyone who

might be suitable to take on a role working with three of our major accounts on the design and development of their next generation of products – potential business to us of about £20 million over the average life of each product. The first name to come to mind was that of Nicky. Nicky and I spent some time working together shortly after we both graduated and we have kept in touch since. Nicky is particularly adept at handling people and getting her own way – and, since these seemed to be the essential requirements for the role the MD had in mind, I recommended her straight away.

So it was with the MD's blessing that I arranged to meet Nicky for lunch. Everything went well until Nicky started talking about the kind of salary she would be looking for. My jaw dropped: she stated a figure £10k a year more than I get after ten years' service with the firm plus the fact I am on the board of management. I know the MD wanted me to be flexible about salary because of the importance of the job, but Nicky's aspirations were way over the top and I told her so. As it seemed we had reached an impasse we left it at that and I reported back to the MD that I had drawn a blank.'

Whether with £20 million's worth of business in the balance, the MD would have viewed Nicky's salary aspirations as over the top or not is a matter for speculation. The decision, as it happened, was not taken by him but by someone exercising a very personal view of what was acceptable. The lesson? Avoid negotiating with anyone who might see the outcome as impinging on his or her own rank, status, privileges and/or salary differentials. Essentially this means beware of peer groups and – if you sense yourself getting into situations like Nicky's, try to stall on pay and perks negotiations till you get to talk to someone higher up the ladder.

File searchers

Don't expect consultants doing 'file search only' assignments to have too much influence over their clients' ideas on pay and perks. Though situations vary, this is not the way it normally works. But what is of interest for you with file search is the fact that it is mostly carried out on a 'no placement, no fee' basis – meaning, once you've got past the hurdles placed by the competition, there is a great incentive on the consultant to smooth the way forward. If he or she fails in this, then all the work has been in vain. Unfortunately, though, this situation does not come without dangers.

'I found myself being pressurised into taking a job that wasn't really right for me. Frankly, the impression I got was that the headhunter was putting his fee in front of my best interests.'

Where the financial rewards are all or nothing it would be a very perfect world where no conflicts of interest ever arose and it is realistic and sensible to expect this.

Despite this high level of interest in positive outcomes, file searchers tend to have an ambivalent attitude towards candidates who seek to negotiate the package upwards.

'In a case I am currently dealing with, a company is prepared to offer a candidate a salary of £30k, but the candidate wants to stick out for another £5k on top. With this client we charge a standard fee of 18% of

starting salary meaning that on £30k we would make a fee of £5,400. On £35k we would make an extra £900 which, while not being something we would turn our noses up at, carries the risk of the client saying no and us ending up with nothing.'

For these reasons expect consultants working on a 'no placement, no fee' basis to feel nervous about trying to negotiate the package upwards. Expect them too to be warning you that you could be pushing your luck. With your bargaining strength potentially at its lowest with file search, take on board that they could be right.

Search and selection consultants

These are the consultants who wear more than one hat – for example, consultants who source candidates from their files then go on to provide clients with assistance in the selection process, e.g. with preliminary interviews, selection tests etc. Like proper search consultants, expect these multi-hatted consultants to give their clients a fair amount of input in the design and delivery of the salary and perks package.

Most headhunters are on your side

What emerges from this overview of headhunters and what is worth reflecting on, is that in most cases:

• they won't be hostile to you seeking to negotiate a good deal for yourself. In some instances it could even be said that they will be 'on your side'

- they will be in a position of influence with the companies who are their clients.

The exceptions are:

- consultants retained on a 'file search only' basis
- company headhunters with a potential axe to grind (better for you to do your negotiating with someone else).

With these exceptions, the path is there for you to open your negotiation with the company by using the headhunter as a conduit. This has three further advantages for you.

- the headhunter knows the company and its culture better than you do, hence he or she will be better placed to judge whether your ideas on pay and perks are going to be seen as 'over the top', i.e. dismissed out of hand with no counter-proposal', meaning negotiation stalls before it gets started and you achieve nothing

- the headhunter will have a better idea than you of where the company's flexibility is constrained by comparators and where seeking to negotiate above certain figures is largely pointless (where perhaps the assessment of your bargaining strength needs to be revised)

- your ideas will sound better coming from the headhunter first and will carry the headhunter's silent endorsement.

How do you proceed with a headhunter?

- **Be straight.** Tell him or her that you are seeking to negotiate the best possible deal for yourself. The headhunter will find nothing strange or reproachable in this.

- **Be ambitious.** Go for what you think you are worth. Don't fall into the trap of asking for too little then finding when the job's offered to you that the salary and perks are not enough. Also, if the company's ideas are below your expectations, it is best to find this out at the beginning.

- **Be clear.** Name your price. Avoid statements that could mean anything like 'I'm earning £x per annum now and I would need a good increase to see my way clear to making a move.' Don't leave something as important as pay and perks open to interpretation. Keep control of the message.

- **Be confident.** Don't start by negotiating with yourself and toning your ideas down to conform with some preconceived idea on what might or might not be acceptable. Leave the negotiating to others.

- **Be receptive.** Listen to what the headhunter has got to say on your ideas.

- **Be consensual.** Reach agreement with the headhunter on the start point for your negotiation.

GOLDEN RULE 17

Negotiate.

CONTROLLING THE SELECTION PROCESS

In earlier chapters we looked at what, in approach situations, stands between you and getting the job. We warned in particular not to confuse approaches with offers of employment. There is usually some distance left for you to travel after a headhunter has spoken to you, though exactly how far depends on the nature of the approach and how much competition you are up against (if any). We noted that:

- **With proper search** (unless you have been informed otherwise) it is best to assume that you are not the only person who has been approached. The chances are that there are other faces in the frame, though it is a fairly safe bet they won't be numerous. Having carried out the preliminary soundings with you, one of a proper search consultant's first tasks will be to satisfy himself or herself on your suitability for the position in question. This means you will be put through interviews, selection tests etc. and this will give the headhunter a shortlist of candidates to be put forward to the client. Further interviews with the client will then be necessary.

- **With companies doing their own headhunting** it is not unusual to find that you are the only person to whom an approach has been made (by now you may have confirmation of this fact). Expect the selection process to be compressed in these cases with you moving quickly from your preliminary discussion with the person making the approach to what in effect will be a final interview.

* **With file search** you will probably be one of many candidates put forward for the job. What's more, there is the possibility that the company has approached more than one recruitment consultant, so you could be up against competition from several file searches. In a lot of cases the recruitment consultant will play no further part in selection beyond the preliminary discussions and selection will be entirely down to the company's own procedures. In other cases the consultant (or a consultant) will be retained to provide expertise and advice with selection, e.g. with interviews, tests etc. With file search, at the point you receive the approach the distance that separates you from getting the job will be a little different from that of a candidate who has been sourced by advertising.

Flaws in selection procedures arising from approach

Though headhunters are celebrated for the stringency of their selection methods – and some undoubtedly deserve to have this reputation – what is striking about a lot of these approach situations is that normal selection procedures are by-passed or compressed (subjected to short-cuts).

The worst offenders are:

* companies doing their own headhunting
* companies sourcing candidates from file searches (companies in a hurry).

'The managing director doesn't trust our personnel department to deal with executive appointments. He prefers to get a firm of management selection consultants to send him a batch of cvs then does the interviews himself. In consequence, it is true to say, that we have more demanding selection standards for junior clerical staff than we do for senior managers.'

Common omissions in approach are:

- standard company application forms are not completed – 'We recruited a manager for a multi-site operation then found out after he joined that he couldn't drive. Candidates usually give their driving licence details on their application forms but, because this individual had come to us from a firm of consultants, he hadn't been given one to complete'.

- 'Basic' questions are not asked – 'It came to light soon after a candidate started that he had a serious health problem. Sad though it was, the job we employed him in was highly stressful and completely unsuitable, hence we ended up having to part company. Questions on medical history are a standard part of our preliminary employment interview – the personnel officer has a checklist she goes through. On this occasion, the candidate came to us from a firm of consultants so he didn't go through the normal interviews. The irony was that the consultants spent hours putting him through just about every psychological test in the book!'

- Less appealing aspects of the job are not mentioned – 'A new senior executive

complained that she had not been told at
interview that one of her key functions
was soon to be removed as part of a
reorganisation of management
responsibilities. At first we did not
understand her complaint as the
reorganisation and its ramifications had
figured prominently in the briefing we
gave to the consultants who were
responsible for headhunting her. When
we asked the consultants to explain, the
answer we got was surprising. They
regarded it as our responsibility to pass on
information such as this, they said – not
theirs!'

• Areas of potential difficulty not explored –
'Soon after starting, a freshly headhunted
candidate told us that he had received a
letter from his ex-employer's solicitors
advising him that they would be starting
legal proceedings against him if he
continued to work for us. It transpired he
was subject to a restrictive covenant
preventing him from joining anyone else
in the industry for a period of at least
two years. When we spoke to the
consultants who recruited him they
clearly had little idea what we were
talking about and didn't seem inclined to
get involved.'

Unclear lines on who is responsible for what.
Consultants too focused on selling jobs to
candidates rather than applying proper selection standards. Companies assuming candidates fished out of a file search have gone
through rigorous selection procedures. Companies not being sufficiently questioning
about the skills of the consultants they are

using. Whatever the problems, the concerns are not just for companies. In each of these situations an unfortunate individual has been pitched into a difficult set of circumstances by what most of us would view as a lapse from normal everyday good selection practice.

So what are the lessons here? Approach, as we have seen, is something we have got to be prepared to live with and encourage if we wish to take advantage of some of the better opportunities that the job market has to offer. 'Live with' means live with:

- headhunters who try to sell you the job rather than give you the full facts

- headhunters whose competence is questionable and who don't know the right questions to ask

- headhunters who are more focused on their commissions than they are on your long-term happiness in a job

- companies who rely on such headhunters.

Don't, whatever you do, run away with the idea that all headhunters fall into one of these categories, because you will be making the mistake of damning the many with the failings of the few. The message here is simply this: see the difficulties that can arise in approach situations and avoid them, once again, by *keeping control*.

Applied to the selection process, keeping control means:

- setting out your stall at the outset as we advised you to do back on page 99. This includes telling the headhunter if you see any difficulties in the way of you getting the job (e.g. you don't drive or you have a health problem, or you are subject to an employment condition like a restrictive covenant or a long period of notice)

- ensuring (by asking the headhunter to confirm) that information such as this has been passed on to the company

- irrespective of the answer to the above, ensuring that the same information is repeated when you get to see the company

- seeking to see if the company does have a standard application form and, if so, offering to complete one

- giving the headhunter a copy of your cv; doing the same with the company

- fishing for the snags by asking the headhunter and the company if there are special challenges or areas of difficulty that you ought to know about

- spotting the omissions (the questions they haven't asked you or where you seem to lack in basic information on the job).

By this piece of keeping control you will have ensured that:

- selection is not proceeding on misreadings of you and your situation

- the headhunter or the company is not under the false impression that the other party has imparted some vital item of information to you

- hitches are not discovered till the last minute or, worse still, till after you have started in the job.

SEEING OFF COMPETITION

Before you can move forward with your negotiation you need to get the job and, with the exception of those situations where you are the only runner in the race, getting the job means seeing off competition.

Strong points

What is always interesting to find out about getting headhunted is 'Why me?' The answer nearly always is that you have some attribute the company headhunting you is very keen to acquire. You have a talent, skill, item of know-how, contacts (or combination of these things) that the company places a high value on and which in turn is the source of your bargaining strength.

By now you will have hopefully learned what it is that the company prizes so highly and, if so, you will also have identified what, in any competitive selection process, are your *strong points*.

Strong points are important. Strong points are what you focus on and use to fight the competition. Take Millie as an example.

CASE STUDY: MILLIE

Millie is a high-flying sales executive working in the advertising industry. Millie has received an approach from a headhunter acting on behalf of another advertising company, a relative newcomer, seeking to extend its client base into recruitment advertising. Millie worked in recruitment advertising for a number of years although her recent experience has been in developing sales to companies in the financial services sector. Millie's strong point as far as this particular approach is concerned is therefore her experience in recruitment advertising. Even though it isn't current it is what she should be focusing on when she is interviewed by the company. They will want to hear about this, together with the extent to which her recruitment advertising experience measures up to that of other candidates, and this will largely determine whether she gets the job or not.

As far as interviews are concerned, focusing on strong points means:

- maximising the time you spend talking about them
- minimising the time you spend talking about anything else.

This is a further example of the principle of *keeping control*. In this case you are keeping control of the messages that flow from you to the interviewer. You are making sure that the bulk of what the interviewer hears is what he or she is tuned in to pick up as a strong qualifying point for the job.

Tapping into the headhunter's knowledge

Given the general unpredictability of interviews, a useful tip for candidates who have been headhunted is to tap into the headhunter's knowledge of the person doing the interviewing, thereby giving yourself a measure of what to expect. Some headhunters will volunteer this information without being prompted, whereas others will have to be asked. You will find that some headhunters have worked with companies for many years so they know the interviewing style well, including any tendency to ask offbeat questions (and the answers that you will be expected to give). Don't miss out on this very privileged source of information. It could serve you well.

> 'I was paraded into an interview where the entire board of directors sat on the other side of a big, long table and fired questions at me one after the other for nearly two hours. Fortunately the headhunter warned me that this would happen. She also told me some of the questions they would ask.'

Occasionally you will find that headhunters sit in on interviews or even chair interviewing panels. In such situations be attuned to picking up where the headhunter is coming to your rescue. This will usually manifest itself in the headhunter putting a question to you that is supplementary to a question that has just been asked by someone else, or asking you to clarify something you have just said. The prompt is for you to insert a point you have omitted to say or to repair some damage you have inflicted on yourself.

....

MOVING THE NEGOTIATION FORWARD (NEGOTIATING WITH THE COMPANY)

We left negotiation at the stage where you had:

- assessed your bargaining power and found it to be strong
- broached your ideas with the headhunter
- listened to the feedback – notably any feedback on how the headhunter viewed

the company's flexibility and willingness to negotiate
- 'agreed' the figure you should be asking for (the figure the headhunter will be taking back to the company).

The negotiation will

- either be continued in your meetings/ interviews with the company
- or left to the end, i.e. to when you are offered the job.

Sticking to your guns in negotiation

There is a chance that going in with a figure that is on the high side will frighten the company off. In this case, should you be watering your aspirations down?

Though companies who regard your talents, skills etc. as sought-after will not be inclined to view you as avaricious, this is one of the reasons for advising you to broach your ideas with the headhunter first. The headhunter serves as a very good test of the temperature of the water and, because he or she won't want you falling at the first hurdle, you will get the tip-off if your ideas are going to cause problems. What you might expose, in the process, is that the company is not as flexible and willing to negotiate as you first thought – meaning your bargaining strength is not as you originally saw it (back to the drawing board with this!).

CASE STUDY: DOMINIC

'A few months ago I was approached about joining a family owned business as its managing director – a move I viewed as intrinsically risky. In salary terms, bearing in mind that I would be leaving a reasonably secure job and taking a plunge into the unknown, I felt I should be asking for a figure of around £80k (I currently earn £65k). I bounced this off the headhunter who shook his head and said he thought £70–£72k was as far as they would stretch. Reluctantly I agreed to lower my sights, then realised my mistake when the job was offered me at a salary of £70k plus another £2k at the end of the year. I saw immediately that I would be taking a risk at a time in my life when my financial outgoings happened to be substantial and all for another £5k a year. The upshot? I turned the job down. I think I did right.'

If Dominic felt this way, he undoubtedly did do right but, by agreeing to one figure then changing his mind when the job was offered to him, he gave the impression of being someone who gets cold feet or who vacillates (not the kind of person a headhunter is keen to deal with). The likely outcome? Dominic won't be getting any more approaches from this particular headhunter.

However, the main object lesson to be drawn from Dominic's tale is to stick to your guns and not be swayed into lowering your negotiating position to an unacceptable level either to be accommodating or to adapt to what is being presented to you as 'the realities'. There is no point at all in putting yourself through a selection procedure then finding at the end of it that the salary you're offered is not enough, and most candidates who find themselves in this position only have themselves to blame.

The advice to Dominic? Next time this happens point out to the headhunter at the outset that taking a big risk for an extra £5k a year makes poor sense. Headhunters will quickly grasp the point and they may even be able to suggest ways of improving the pay or reducing the risk (e.g. the kind of soft landing we will be talking about later in this chapter). Failing this, Dominic's relationship with the headhunter is still intact. Furthermore the headhunter now has a better idea of where Dominic is coming from so the next approach he gets stands a chance of being more to his liking (more money or less risk).

Fishing for the company's best offer

The term 'negotiate' tends to conjure up images of smoke-filled rooms and the kind of negotiating between trade unions and employers that filled the pages of our newspapers back in the 1970s. One side moved its offers slowly upwards while the other watched and waited for the gap to close on its demands.

Negotiating the packages of executives who have been headhunted isn't like this. For a start, any negotiating tends to be compressed. Example:

> Company A wishes to headhunt Jane B. Jane B has flagged up to the headhunter that she is looking for £50k. Company A wasn't expecting to have to pay £50k for Jane B's talents; a figure of £40k is more like what they had in mind. Company A is therefore effectively left with two choices:

> • pay Jane B the £50k she is asking for
> • offer £40k and run the risk she will decline.

Which of these two choices Company A goes for depends ultimately on how highly they value Jane B's talents. In other words, by putting Company A on the spot Jane B is testing her bargaining strength.

Let's now take the example a little further. Let's say Company A decides it can't offer Jane B £50k because it would put her on a higher salary than her boss is on. Let's say that this is the reason why they choose to offer £40k and run the risk of her saying no. What Jane B has done is to plumb the depths of her bargaining strength. She now knows how far it stretches and can be reasonably sure (as sure as she can ever be in these situations) that £40k is Company A's 'best offer'. She must now decide whether to accept or decline. Before she declines, however there is one last avenue to explore.

....

ENHANCING THE PACKAGE

Where you approach the point of impasse with a company because the salary they are offering isn't enough it is useful to try and find out what is holding them back. You mustn't rule out, of course, that they don't attach sufficient value to your talents to pay you the kind of salary you are looking for and this reflects back on your bargaining strength – or lack of it. Nine times out of ten, however, the impasse arises not because the company doesn't rate what you have to offer highly enough but because it is constrained in what it can do by internal pay comparators. Company A is a case in point. Company A was very keen to headhunt Jane B but offering her the salary she was looking for would have put her above the figure Company A pays to her boss.

Understandably Company A felt it couldn't do this.

The first difficulty for Jane B is that Company A may not tell her why they can't pay her £50k. They may feel uneasy about discussing internal salary structures with her and, as a consequence, Jane B (like many others put in the same position) may come away feeling the conflict is with the company's culture. 'They're poor payers' is a common observation made by Jane Bs.

How does Jane B find out what's holding Company A back? The answer is to ask the headhunter. The headhunter has a very direct interest in the outcome of the approach and he or she will be making it his or her business to find out why the negotiation is floundering. If it is a problem with salary comparators the headhunter may be able to come to the rescue, e.g. by finding out what the constraints are and then seeking to drive a bargain between the parties (a last ditch attempt).

But failing this, what might be worth exploring is whether there is any mileage in:

- titillating the non salary items in the package (i.e. the perks)
- paying a 'golden hello'.

Before going on to consider these options, let's ask ourselves what we are seeking to do here. The company has a problem with comparators but there are no other obstacles in the way of the approach (e.g. they have no reservation about you or what you have to offer them). The object is therefore to redesign the package so that:

- it will be acceptable to you
- it won't give the same problems as a package that is biased towards salary items.

Perks

The perks industry took off in the UK during the various phases of statutory pay restraint that we had in the 1970s. Companies sought ways other than through the pay packet for rewarding key employees. Thus the range of perks that used to consist of the superannuation scheme and the Christmas turkey blossomed into cars and share options then into bigger and better cars, spouses' cars, private healthcare, help with the children's school fees ... till the list today has become practically endless, meaning somewhere there has to be a perk or package of perks that has special significance for you. So, for example, if you're single, foot-loose and fancy-free, a sporty little convertible might be worth more than the extra pounds in salary. If you and your spouse both lead busy lives, then help with the domestics may be more on the agenda.

Golden hellos

Just in case you are unfamiliar with the term, these are large up-front sums paid to new recruits when they join. The payment is either a one-off or it is made in instalments and sometimes there is provision for a clawback of all or part of the golden hello in the event of the employee's premature departure. Golden hellos are largely (though not exclusively) associated with senior executive appointments and it is common to find them used in approach situations. While the enticement value of golden hellos is substantial another reason for their use is that they don't give problems with internal salary structures. Example:

*Company C wishes to headhunt a new
partner (John D). John D is a partner in a
rival business. He earns £60k which is also
what Company C pays to its partners. Paying
John D any more than £60k will give
Company C problems. Answer: they offer John
D £60k plus a £50k golden hello to make
the move worth his while.*

Because of the tendency towards flatter company structures a lot of senior executive moves these days are effectively sideways and golden hellos enable companies to make these sideways moves financially attractive.

The suggestion that the impasse you have reached with a company over salary could be overcome with perks and/or golden hellos is probably best put to them by the headhunter. The headhunter, in most cases, will be expected to give the company input on pay and perks packages whereas you doing the same could be viewed with suspicion. If the company is unfamiliar with golden hellos or imaginative perks, the suspicion could turn into outright hostility. In short, you achieve nothing and the impasse sticks.

Snags? Some companies will back off at the mention of custom-made perks and golden hellos. This is not just a question of being fuddy-duddy, their objections are often practical ones, as the following quotes illustrate.

*'In our experience nothing causes more
trouble than company cars. I can well
imagine some newcomer turning up in a
fancy sports coupe and us having a riot of
the senior management team on our hands.'*

*'Try justifying a golden hello to someone who
didn't get one. I can see us ending up having
to pay everyone golden hellos.'*

*'We would be a sitting target for people with
no long-term interest in the company. They
would pocket the golden hello then be off
again at the first chance they got.'*

One of the advantages of working closely with
the headhunter is that he or she will be able to
warn you off if the suggestion to overcome an
impasse by enhancing the package with non-
salary items is likely to run into a brick wall.

....

DEALING WITH ENTICEMENT

At the back of most approach is a company
very keen to acquire your particular blend of
experience and skills. Often this keenness
manifests itself in the company making the
running in the negotiation, culminating in an
offer you will find hard to refuse. Sounds
good? In a lot of cases it will mean you have
hit the jackpot but what you must never do in
these situations is to let the glitter of gold get
in the way of your better judgement. A bad
move is still a bad move irrespective of how it
is dressed up.

*'I knew I was making a mistake but how do
you say no to an extra £10k, the kind of car
you've only ever dreamed about and a
£50,000 golden hello?'*

The answer is, it's hard but say no is what you
must do if all the warning signs are flashing at
you that you are about to make a bad move.
The justification? The extra pay and perks
won't do you much good if the job only lasts
six months. The golden hello won't seem so
wonderful when the company is seeking to

claw it back (or if only a part of it ever found its way into your pocket). Bad moves, furthermore, are hard to repair. In some cases it means you having to make an emergency escape (taking the first alternative job that comes along). In others it means being out of work or having to take a step down. It could be years before you get your career back on track and you need to consider this. The words 'I knew I was making a mistake ...' are fairly typical and victims of enticement are often guilty of not listening to their inner voices.

GOLDEN RULE 18

All offers are refusable.

....

MINIMISING THE RISKS

When you receive an approach the question is always lurking somewhere in the back of your mind – 'What happens if this doesn't work out?'

Risk is inherent in every job move and, as such, it is best addressed as a reality. This means don't do as a lot of candidates do and divide your approaches into the two extremes – risky and risk free. Risk free doesn't exist. Moreover, the factors that can lead to a job not working out for you often don't manifest themselves until some time after you have started. The clash of personalities, the constraints placed on what you can and can't do, the office politics – there is no way you will have these sussed out at the time you have to make the decision on whether to take the job or not.

Approach has two further problems for those who feel nervous about taking a leap into the unknown:

- It frequently comes at you when you are not active on the job market – when you are quite happy with what you are doing and have no clear reason for wanting to leave. On the one hand, you can't turn your back on what could be the chance of a lifetime; on the other, why should you be taking a risk when you don't have to?

- With some forms of approach, selection processes are compressed (as we have seen) so everything happens so much more quickly and the period of time between receiving the approach and being asked to make your mind up hardly seems long enough to get used to the idea of embarking on a new chapter in your career.

Assessing the risks

Rather than sweating over questions you don't have the answers to, risk is best put to a two-part test:

First, see that every risk has two sides to it – an upside and a downside. With a job the downside is pretty obvious – you make a bad move and you have to face the consequences. The upside, however, varies. At one end of the scale, the job could be a barely discernible move upwards with a few extra frills. At the other, it could represent a major step forward in your career. The point is this: risks with a big upside are worth taking; those that don't have a big upside need thinking about.

Second, ask yourself the extent to which you

can afford to take risks. For example, if you are unemployed with few outgoings and no responsibilities other than for yourself, there should be nothing to hold you back. On the other hand, if you're heavily mortgaged and the sole breadwinner for a family then you need to err on the cautious side.

Negotiating soft landings

Given, however, that you are taking a step into the unknown (who knows how it will turn out?) approach and the bargaining strength that so often goes with it presents you with an opportunity to negotiate some soft landings if the worst should ever come to the worst.

With top executive packages, the soft landing could be a so-called golden parachute, where specified amounts of compensation become payable in the event of your contract being terminated. It would be usual to find the terms of such an arrangement enshrined in a service agreement and, because of the large cash sums involved and the ferocity with which they might be contested at some point in the future, it is advisable to get a lawyer's eye cast over the wording before you sign on the dotted line.

> 'Ten months into the job, the company was sold and the new owners decided they wanted all the existing senior management team out. There was no offer of compensation and we were left to fight our own cases. Thank goodness that I had a clause in my service agreement spelling out my entitlements. After some preliminary quibbling, the new owners paid out in full.'

Yet, as a general observation, we find that in recruitment situations the subject of risk does not receive sufficient attention either by companies or by those they are seeking to employ. There is nothing sinister about this disregard (most companies won't be harbouring dark thoughts about cutting their losses in the event of you failing in the job). The plain truth is far simpler. It is that at the time of making the appointment, neither party is contemplating any outcome other than its success. You will be confident in your ability to do the job just as the company will have every faith it has made the right choice. Sadly, however, when things don't work out, you are left with nothing to fall back on other than your contractual notice period.

> 'Out of the blue, our parent company in Switzerland decided to pull out of the UK market. Since I didn't have the service to qualify for a redundancy payment, all I got was three months' salary in lieu of notice.'

The suggestion we are putting before you is to use your bargaining strength in approach situations to get some term inserted in your contract so that you are covered in the event of things not working out. Under pressure from institutional shareholders, companies have been reluctant in recent years to put employees on long rolling periods of notice (the normal safeguard that you would be walking out with a reasonable sum in your pocket if the company decided to terminate your employment abruptly).

So what do you need to do?

- Start with your friendly headhunter again. Raise the subject of risk – not because you have any qualms about your ability to do the job, but because risk is always a factor when you move from one company to another. Get the headhunter to see the point.

- Explore the possibility of the company offering contractual compensation terms or extended rolling notice periods. Get the headhunter to do this for you.

- If you draw a blank (because what you are suggesting is contrary to company policy) propose an arrangement where your employment would be guaranteed for a fixed term at the start (with senior executive positions, two to three years would not seem unreasonable). This acknowledges the fact that the riskiest period of any job is at the beginning.

....

MOVING INTO THE FUTURE WITH HEADHUNTERS

Time and time again in this book we have drawn attention to the importance of your relationship with the headhunter. We have shown how headhunters can:

- tell you where you stand in selection
- smooth the path for you and make your dealings with companies easier
- tell you why you have been approached and enable you to identify your strong points
- help you to negotiate a good deal for yourself
- put you wise to situations where the company may have constraints on its flexibility and willingness to negotiate
- help you steer the way round impasses

- give you inside information.

Throughout approach you can draw on the headhunters' knowledge of the company and his or her unique access to decision makers.

Developing a good relationship with a head-hunter is something you have to work on. You do this by:

- making yourself available to them (having that one phone call contactability)
- going back to them when you say you will and not leaving them to chase you
- being straight with them
- being consistent (not saying one thing then changing your mind later on)
- listening to any advice they give you
- not letting their clients down.

Into the last category comes attending interviews that headhunters arrange for you. Not all candidates attend their interviews and some forget to cancel or apologise. Needless to say, companies on the receiving end of such treatment feel put out and the person most likely to catch it in the neck is the poor headhunter. Don't expect forgiveness from headhunters if you fail to turn up for interviews and don't expect them to give you any second chances to let down their clients. If you find you can't make an interview for any reason then get on to the headhunter straight away. Try to avoid doing this at the last minute because the headhunter still has to make contact with the company.

Hopefully your experience of getting head-hunted will be a fruitful one and you will end up with the kind of job you've always dreamt about. Don't, however, let your relationship with the headhunter end there. You still have the most exacting challenge in front of you (making a success of your new job) and you are entering a period where you still need to have all your options open. Though we hope you don't have need of the headhunter's services sooner than you expected, it is comforting to know that a source of good jobs is only a phone call away. Moving further into the future, you have the next step in your career to consider, so being on the headhunter's net and being available to his or her calls is something you should seek to develop.

Two other ways in which you can move into the future with headhunters are as follows:

- From time to time they may want to tap into your bank of knowledge for the names of potential candidates for other assignments that land on their desks. Be as helpful as you can. If someone who could be of interest to them is known to you even offer your services as a go-between.

- If in your new job you are responsible for employing people, remember the headhunter and pass some business his or her way.

GOLDEN RULE 19

Cultivate headhunters.

REASONS FOR APPROACHES NOT TURNING INTO JOBS

Not all approaches are going to work out for you and you shouldn't expect them to. Nevertheless if you find you are receiving approaches regularly but the approaches don't turn into jobs the following checklist might help you to put your finger on where the trouble lies:

- Are your approaches all the result of file search? If so, the reasons for your lack of success could range from poor matching of candidates through to sheer weight of competition. Don't agonise too much over this (it is mostly outside your control). Concentrate instead on trying to drum up approaches from proper search consultants and companies doing their own headhunting.

- Are the approaches for jobs that don't interest you? There are two probable explanations here: either the headhunters aren't reading you correctly (answer: educate them) or what does interest you is confined to a very narrow and limited field (answer: think again). Beware too that you are not setting your sights too high (overreaching) or that the job you are looking for doesn't exist (commoner than you think). Bounce your ideas off the headhunters and get their opinions.

- Are you being passed over in favour of other candidates? Go back to what we had to say about strong points (pages 137 to 138). Are you identifying strong points correctly? If so, are you bringing them sufficiently to the fore in your interviews? Again, make sure the approaches are not all generated from file search where the reason for your lack of success may not be connected to anything you are getting wrong.

- Are the salaries you are being offered not coming up to your expectations? This suggests poor transmission of your ideas, but is that from you or from the headhunter? If you are having the same problem with different headhunters, then the blame probably lies at your door. The usual cause here is lack of clarity: don't wrap up your salary expectations in woolly statements; name the figure you want to see on the table. If you suspect the headhunter is at fault, try exercising more control and ask the headhunter to tell you what messages have been fed to the company; challenge anything you feel is misrepresentational.

If an approach doesn't work out your main area of concern is keeping the relationship with headhunters sweet so the approaches keep coming. A danger in backing out of approaches or turning offers down is that headhunters will see you as indecisive or difficult to please and as a result you could find your approaches start to dry up. The message is get to the bottom of what's going wrong and involve the headhunter so your concern and determination to put matters right is evident.

GOLDEN RULE 20

Build on experience.

Questions and answers

Asking for more money to compensate for risk

Q The closer I am to getting this particular job, the more I realise that the risks are bigger than I thought. Should I be asking for more money to compensate for these risks? If so, how do I broach the subject with the head-hunter?

A You are right to anticipate that changing your ideas on salary will require some explaining to the headhunter. Unless you do it properly there is a danger the headhunter will see you as going back on your word and you could be seen as a difficult person to deal with. There is a more fundamental issue here, however. You can never buy-off risk. Apart from anything else, if the job doesn't work out, the extra salary you will have earned during your short stay will only amount to peanuts. It is better to view risk in the way we suggested back on pages 149 to 150. See what the upsides are, assess your capacity to take the risks then, if the signals still say go, negotiate a contractual soft landing for yourself.

Bargaining strength and the unemployed

Q As an unemployed person, what bargaining strength do I have? Won't employers offer me the lowest salary they think they can get away with knowing that I am hardly likely to say no?

A We understand what you are saying, though some mileage can probably be gained from creating the impression that there are other employers who are interested in you. But no, don't jeopardise your chances of getting back into employment by arguing over the finer points of the salary. That would be silly. A better approach by far would be to get the job first then work on the salary later – that is, achieve your aims one at a time. Another book in the Orion *PowerTools* series,

Thrive in Your Company, by Catt and Scudamore, gives you guidance on how to do this.

Future promises

Q After a fairly protracted negotiation via the headhunter, the company has finally agreed to pay me the salary I am asking for, but only on completion of one year's service. Should I be seeing anything sinister in this?

A Probably not, as nine times out of ten this will simply reflect a company wanting to see you perform before paying you a higher salary (higher, possibly, than some of their existing staff). Admittedly there are companies who make promises that they have no intention of keeping and the desperation that is behind some companies who use the approach route is the reason for this. To prevent yourself becoming the victim of an empty promise, spot those companies who are acting out of desperation and who are likely to be unscrupulous. As a safeguard ask them to put the promise into writing. This is not said with a view to encouraging you to fly off into litigation if the promise doesn't materialise. The intention is, rather, to expose companies who are not prepared to put their promises into writing. The inference you can fairly safely draw is that they have no intention of carrying their promises out.

TICK YOUR PROGRESS
....

✓ Getting headhunted means you have something a company is prepared to pay for. Don't sell yourself short by failing to negotiate.

✓ Beware of trying to negotiate when you

have little or no bargaining power. Only seek to strike deals from positions of strength.

✓ Let headhunters make the running for you. Take advantage of the interest they have in bringing the approach to a successful conclusion.

✓ Keep headhunters on your side. Don't let seeking to get a good deal come across as you being unreasonable or difficult to please.

✓ Keep control of the selection process. Make sure that nothing vital is omitted.

✓ Overcome competition by identifying your strong points and bringing them to the fore.

✓ Keep your pay aspirations up though agree with the headhunter where your negotiations should start.

✓ Seek to overcome impasses by converting your aspirations into non-salary items (perks) or golden hellos. Back off when you see you are banging your head on a brick wall.

✓ Watch out for companies driven by desperation who make you offers they think you won't be able to refuse. Recognise that approach and enticement often come together.

✓ Only take risks you can afford to take and where the upsides are big enough. Recognise that there is always a risk.

✓ Face up to the possibility of the job not working out. Use the bargaining strength you have in approach to negotiate a soft landing for yourself.

✓ Move into the future with headhunters. Seek to keep the approaches coming.

✓ Build on the experience you get from each approach. Get better at dealing with headhunters and capitalising on the opportunities that are put in front of you.

Part five

GET HEADHUNTED – A MODEL APPROACH

....

MARKETING YOURSELF TO HEADHUNTERS

- Work hard on your work perfect and person perfect image. Whatever your flaws are, don't broadcast them – especially to your colleagues.

- Use your contacts to access proper search consultants. Play these people at their own game.

- Work on having a public profile that projects beyond your company. Associate yourself with any success your company has had.

- Keep active on the job market. Keep your name on consultants' files and make sure the information they are holding on you is up to date.

- Don't view dealing with firms of recruitment consultants as a chore. Help them to help you.

- Identify key areas of your skills and experience. Bring these to the fore in the messages you feed out to consultants.

- Pay attention to your availability. Make sure headhunters trying to get hold of you don't meet with barriers.

....

HANDLING APPROACHES

- View your approaches objectively. Listen to everything you are told, get facts and make your judgements accordingly.

- Make headhunters welcome. Be polite to them and always hear out what they've got to say. Never shut the door in a headhunter's face.

- Keep approaches to yourself. Don't succumb to the temptation to tell your colleagues and friends.

- Be aware of approaches that pose a threat to you. Approaches from competitors come under this heading.

- Keep your approaches under control. Take responsibility for ensuring that selection procedures are followed properly. Don't let the speed at which events move or omissions by headhunters get you into a mess.

- Keep the approaches coming. Don't do anything to put headhunters off you. Don't let your approach become a one-off event.

....

GETTING THE BEST DEAL

- See where your bargaining strengths lie. Never negotiate from a position of weakness.

- Use headhunters to test the temperature

of the water for you. Listen to any advice they have to give.

- Have confidence in your ability to drive a good bargain.

- Let headhunters act as the go-between for you. Use the influence they have with their clients along with the interest they have in bringing the approach to a successful conclusion.

- Put yourself in the position of preferred candidate by identifying and pushing your strong points. Let companies see that you are worth what you are asking for.

- Assess the risks. Let your willingness to take risks be determined by the size of the upsides and your ability to live with the downsides. Use the bargaining strength you have in approach to negotiate some soft landings for yourself.

- Be on the lookout for companies who are desperate (companies who might resort to enticement). Don't let getting headhunted be the reason for you making a bad move.

THE GOLDEN
RULES

Rule 1.
See what's in it for you

Being a target for headhunters' approaches puts you in line for some of the best jobs (and the ones for which there is least competition). Don't miss out on this.

The best jobs are never advertised, so they say, and the evidence of the growth of the so-called invisible job market is all around us: jobs that, to a large extent, are filled by approaches either from companies direct or from firms of consultants acting on behalf of companies. The message here is simple: don't miss out on this valuable source of opportunities by failing to acknowledge its existence. Instead cultivate your ability to get head-hunted and, if you're looking to move up in the world, see getting yourself on the head-hunters' nets as more important to you than scanning the job ads in the newspaper (you will be doing both, of course).

Rule 2.
Cultivate your networks

Most approaches come, directly or indirectly, from people who know you and the quality of your work. Pay attention to impressions you create – particularly among your colleagues and professional contacts.

Rule 3.
Be visible

Take every opportunity to get your name in information which is in the public domain.

Hiding your light under a bushel will do nothing to add to your chances of being headhunted, whereas any visibility you can strike up outside your own company will help you more than you think.

Headhunters frequently resort to information that is either at their fingertips or brought to their attention by other means. This is why, if you are serious about getting headhunted, you should seize every opportunity that comes your way to:

- get your name in any document that might find its way into the public domain, e.g. marketing fliers, company newsletters, entries in trade directories, advertisements etc.

- broadcast your achievements. For example have you ever thought of a press release on any aspects of your work that are newsworthy? (Warning: unless your job brief includes the authority to issue press releases do remember to get your company's consent – chief executives understandably get tetchy when they first hear of something that's going on from reading it in the newspaper!)

- get yourself in on the act if your company is doing anything that is likely to get media coverage

- take a leading part in bodies such as professional institutions, business groups and trade associations.

Rule 4.
Market yourself effectively

Get your name on headhunters' files. Use your skills and experience to sell yourself.

Getting headhunted should not be seen as a chance event over which you have little or no control, but the outcome of having personal aims and strategies that key into the market that headhunting serves. In this, the pursuit of talent and scarce skills should never be underrated for it is the feed pipe to the headhunter's trade – a fundamental part of their *raison d'être*. So, in seeking to get yourself headhunted, your success will depend, not just on cultivating your networks and ensuring your visibility, but also on how good you are at marketing your talents and skills – in particular how good you are at fetching these talents and skills into prominence on the databases that headhunters use.

Rule 5.
Add to your value

Enhance your chances of being headhunted by increasing and perfecting the range of your skills and experience.

In terms of your ability to draw the attentions of headhunters, the more complete your range of experience and skills, the more attractive a target you will provide. Never miss a chance to add to your value. Never miss a chance to do anything unusual that will add to your scarcity.

Rule 6.
Be available

Make it easy for headhunters to get hold of you, so don't miss out on chances because you're not there to take the calls. Headhunters won't waste time on people who are difficult to contact on the telephone.

Rule 7.
Be prepared

Don't let the suddenness with which head-hunters approach you sweep you off your feet. In particular, don't shut down an approach before it gets off the ground by negative off-the-cuff comments that are not properly thought out. Be prepared for the mystery callers but only speak to them when you are ready. Keep control. (Also see Rule 13.)

Rule 8.
Don't close doors

Always hear out what a headhunter has got to say to you.

We live in a world that is changing rapidly and where advancing your career is no longer a matter of sticking with one company till the prospects dry up then firing off dozens of job applications in the hope that sooner or later something good will come along. When you think about it, the chances of you clicking with the right move during one of these short intense periods of job market activity are pretty remote, so small surprise that so many moves turn out to be bad moves. Contrast this with a more on-going approach to planning

your career moves – one in which you con-
stantly have your eye to what the outside
world has to offer and where you are viewing
opportunities as and when they arise – then
the important part that headhunters can play
becomes apparent. So, no, don't turn your
back on headhunters. Hear out what they've
got to say every time they phone.

Rule 9.
Don't be dazzled

Stay detached when you receive an approach.
Don't let the feeling of flattery get the better
of your judgement.

For most of us being at the centre of
attention isn't easy to handle but you must
stand back from approach and see what cards
the headhunter deals you from the pack
before you start getting too excited. Neither
does that fact that a position is being filled by
approach make it special or different from any
other position. Strip off the glamour factor
and judge the job for what it's worth. Bad
companies as well as good companies use
approach and you need to be ready for both.

Rule 10.
Listen

Don't hear headhunters selectively. Take in
everything you are told – not just the things
you want to hear.

Approach is different from applying for
advertised jobs in one very fundamental
respect: the information on which you base
your decision to go forward is imparted to you
orally rather than in written form, hence it is

important that you listen carefully to everything that is said to you.

Rule 11.
Find out where you stand

How the headhunter got your name will tell you how to handle the approach. Ask.

Knowing how to handle an approach and, as you move through the selection process, knowing what to expect next depends on whether you are talking to someone who has pulled your name off a database, a proper search consultant or a company doing its own headhunting. Ask the headhunter at the first possible opportunity and form an opinion from the answer you get.

Rule 12.
Don't confuse approaches with job offers

You still have to go the distance. Don't celebrate yet.

To varying degrees, headhunters are positive people who tend to paint rosy pictures of jobs, companies and people's prospects. So far so good, but when there is the added ingredient of the someone on the receiving end feeling flattered and not listening properly, the danger is there for the approach to be taken as an offer of a job. Always play on the safe side. Don't ever take it that a job is yours until you have the offer in writing in your hands.

Rule 13.
Keep control

Get in the driving seat as soon as you can.

Dictate the course of events and the pace at which they move.

Because it could be 'different' from the method of recruitment a company is used to using, there are dangers in approach for candidates who don't keep control. Questions aren't asked, facts aren't established and approaches can move forward on false and precarious footings. The need is for candidates to take responsibility for ensuring that the steps that are normal in a selection procedure are followed and nothing is left out because of omissions on the company's or the headhunter's parts or because of misunderstandings between them.

Rule 14.
Set out your stall

Let headhunters see where you are coming from. Don't allow the approach to proceed on misunderstandings.

Rule 15.
Keep it to yourself

Along with not confusing approaches with offers, another golden rule is keeping them to yourself. You've not got the job yet and anything could happen ranging from:

- someone else being chosen
- you finding out as the selection process moves on that the job is not for you
- the company deciding not to proceed with its plans to recruit (the vacancy is cancelled or put on ice, e.g. because of changes in the company's trading circumstances).

People are attuned to the idea of keeping quiet about job applications. They realise that it could put them into difficult positions if what they were up to reached their company's ears. Not so, with being headhunted. Because approach is something that is unsolicited, people on the receiving end of it don't see that they have done anything that could lay them open to criticism, and so then tend to talk freely about what has happened to them both to their friends and professional contacts. Companies, however, take a rather different view. Someone who is on a headhunter's net is a risk, a potential short-term stayer, and, because of this fact, the someone in question could find his or her career prospects downgraded or investment in his or her development and training cut back. Unfair? Maybe, but companies are understandably nervous about people who could be off at the drop of a hat.

Don't feed the grapevine by telling colleagues and professional contacts that you have received an approach. If your company is going to find out, let it be from your lips and at a time of your choosing.

Rule 16.
Don't look gift horses in the mouth

Don't let indecision be the reason for you turning down good offers. Opportunity rarely knocks twice.

Getting headhunted means being in a constant state of readiness for making big decisions otherwise you will find yourself passing up good chances for no reason other than hesitancy. Sadly, the problems for you won't end there. Indecisiveness carries two further penalties:

- the chances don't come up again
- headhunters view you as a time-waster, so they get fed up with you and strike you off their lists.

Value your approaches and don't put up the kind of mental barriers that could lead you into turning your back on a job of your dreams.

Rule 17.
Negotiate

Make the most of the chance to get the best possible deal for yourself. Use the headhunter as your go-between.

Getting headhunted offers you a unique opportunity to take a big step forward with your pay and perks:

- the fact someone wants you badly enough to go to the expense and trouble of headhunting you indicates that you have got great bargaining strengths

- the involvement of headhunters provides you with the means to test out how far the company is prepared to go.

Except in situations where your bargaining power is weak, always seek to establish how far you can stretch the company behind an approach.

Rule 18.
All offers are refusable

Beware of bad moves. Don't be talked into taking a job that's not right for you.

Despite all we've had to say about not looking gift horses in the mouth, be on your guard if you feel you are being made an offer you can't refuse. Be especially on your guard if you feel the company or the headhunter is trying to 'sell you the job'. The fact that a company has to resort to hiking up pay and perks just to get you on board is an indicator that they may be desperate. Desperate in turn could mean:

- they are in a mess
- they can't keep staff
- previous applicants have turned them down.

Learn to pick out companies who value good people and reward them well from those who are simply in a jam (where employment prospects will be poor and short-lived). Both sorts tend to use headhunting.

Rule 19.
Cultivate headhunters

Keep on the right side of headhunters. You may be speaking to them again.

Don't view getting headhunted as a one-off event. Aim instead at being on the receiving end of approaches over and over again. Learn to build on your relationships with headhunters so the approaches keep coming. Don't give them any reason for wanting to distance themselves from you.

Rule 20.
Build on experience

Being headhunted is something you get better at. Take on board the lessons you have learned so you are ready for the next time.

INDEX

accessibility 55, 56, 63, 78–9
advertisements 16–17
  search and selection consultants 47–9
application forms 100, 133
approaches 164
  bargaining strength 117–21
  from competitors 103–6, 110–11
  control 174–5
  by ex-employers 110
  finding out where you stand 91–7
  first contact 81–8
  flattery 86–7, 95–6, 173, 174
  handling 77–111, 174
  indecision 116–17, 176–7
  moving forward 97–101
  non-genuine 109
  preparation for 80–5, 172
  reasons for 118
  refusing 97, 106–9
  secrecy 101–6, 110–11, 175–6
  setting out your stall 99–101
  unfruitful 154–6
availability 27, 57–8, 64–72, 79, 172
availability audit 27, 68–70

bargaining strength 117–23, 164–5, 177
  company headhunters 120–1, 125–7
  flexibility 140–3
  proper search consultants 124–5
  unemployed people 157–8

cold calling 33
comfort factor 28, 118, 120
company headhunters 14, 93–4
  bargaining strength 120–1, 125–7
  competition for position 28, 91, 92, 93–4
  direct approaches 27–31
  first contact 80
  negotiating 124–7
  selection process 131–3
  stimulating approaches by 27–31

competition for position 137–9, 155
  bargaining strength 118
  company headhunters 28, 91, 92, 93–4
  file searches 91, 92–3
  proper search consultants 32, 91, 93
competitors to present employers, approaches from
    103–6,110–11
consultants
  see also file search; proper search; recruitment
    consultants; search and selection
  hybrids 47–51
  proper search 31–40
  sources 71–2
  types 14–16
control 63, 174–5
  home telephone availability 67
  moving approach forward 98–101
  negotiability test 108
  selection process 131–6
curriculum vitae
  e-mail address 69
  home telephone availability 64, 65, 67
  one quick read test 78
  proper search consultants 37, 39
  registration forms 52–3

direct approaches 27–31

economy 26
employment agencies 43–4
employment history 26–7
enticement 147–8, 173, 177–8
ex-employers, approaches by 110
executive search and selection consultants 20
experience 26, 171
  key areas 56, 58–63, 79

file search consultants 51–8
  bargaining strength 121
  finding out where you stand 91, 93, 94–5
  first contact 80
  getting onto files of 41–4
  hybrids 47–51
  interviews 62

key areas 56, 58–63
negotiating 127–8
search consultants 47, 52–7
selection process 132
types 15, 42–4
first contact 80–8
first impressions 82
flattery 86–7, 95–6, 173, 174
flexibility
  bargaining strength 119
  salary 84–5, 122–3

golden hellos 144, 145–7
golden parachutes 150–2

headhunters
  see also company headhunters; consultants; file
    search; proper search; recruitment consultants;
    search and selection
  files 171
  interviews with 89–90
  lack of professionalism 70–1
  pestering by 70
  reasons for use of 16–18
  relationship with 82, 85, 106–9, 152–4, 172–3, 178
  setting out your stall 99–101
  sources 71–2
  types 14–16
  types of jobs 19–20
headhunting, reasons for not being 25–7, 77–9
headshunting 109
home, availability at 66–8

indecision 116–17, 176–7
interviews
  with headhunters 89–90
  registration with recruitment consultants 62
  relationship with headhunter 153
  selection process 94–5, 100
  strong points 137–9

jobs, types headhunted for 19–20, 32

key areas 56, 58–63, 79

lifelong interview 27, 31, 34, 78

marketing yourself 63, 163, 171
mobile phones 64, 69

negotiability test 107-9
negotiation 115-58, 164-5, 177
  bargaining strength 117-21
  company headhunters 124-7
  file searchers 127-8
  flattery 87
  flexibility 119
  opening 121-30
  salary expectations 84, 107-8, 140-8
  search and selection consultants 128
networks 30, 78, 169
  see also professional networks; social networks
  lifelong interview 31
  proper searchers 33-4

office, availability at 66
old boy/girl network see social networks
one quick read test 55, 78

pain 119, 120-1, 123
perks 144-7
person perfect test 27, 34, 78, 163
pesterers 70
pestering 70
professional institutions 33, 78
professional networks 30
proper search consultants 14-15
  bargaining strength 120, 124-5
  contacting directly 38-40
  finding out where you stand 91, 93, 94
  first contact 80
  getting onto files of 36-40
  hybrids 47-51
  methods 32-4
  selection process 131
  stimulating approach from 31-6
  type of jobs 19-20
public profile 34-6, 78

recession 26
recruitment consultants
  choice of 44–6
  definition 43
  interviews 62
  registering 46–7
  registration forms 47, 52–7, 62
registration forms 47
  file search consultants 52–7
  key areas 62
  one quick read test 78
résumé *see* curriculum vitae
risk 148–52, 156–7
  secrecy 110–11

salary
  bargaining strength 117–30
  company headhunters 124–5
  first contact 84–5
  flexibility 119
  negotiation 140–8
  proper search consultants 124–5
  risk 156–7
  under-stating 124
  unfruitful approaches 155–6
search consultants 43
  see also proper search
search and selection consultants 20, 43, 47–51
  negotiation 128
secrecy 101–6, 110–11, 175–6
selection consultants 43
selection process 93–5
  company headhunters 93–4, 131–3
  control 131–6, 135–6
  file search 94–5, 132
  proper search 94, 131
self-marketing 63, 163, 171
setting out your stall 99–101
skills 26, 171
  key areas 56, 58–63, 79
snobbery *see* social networks
social networks 37, 71
soft landings 150–2
strong points 137–8

telephone
  availability 64–8
  first contact 81–2
  importance of 40, 64–5
  preparation for calls 82–5
timing 115–16
trade associations 33, 78

unemployed people, bargaining strength 157–8

visibility 34–6, 78, 170

work perfect test 27, 34, 78
workplace availability 65, 66